Historical Memory
versus
Communist Identity

Historical Memory
versus
Communist Identity

Proceedings of the Conference
"The Shaping of Identity and Personality under Communist Rule:
History in the Service of Totalitarian Regimes in Eastern Europe,"
Tallinn, 9–10 June 2011

Edited by Meelis Saueauk

UNIVERSITY OF TARTU
PRESS
1632

The conference "Shaping of Identity and Personality during Communist Rule: History in the Service of the Totalitarian Regimes in Eastern Europe" was hosted on June 9–10, 2011 by the Estonian Institute of Historical Memory and the Unitas Foundation. We would like to thank our partners, supporters, and authors for their contributions towards the conference and this publication.

Organising Committee: Uve Poom (CEO, Unitas Foundation),
　　Toomas Hiio (Member of Board, Estonian Institute of Historical Memory),
　　Meelis Saueauk (Research Fellow, Estonian Institute of Historical Memory).

Estonian Institute of Historical Memory
The Estonian Institute of Historical Memory was established by President Toomas Hendrik Ilves in 2008 in order to provide the citizens of Estonia with a thorough and objective account of the status of human rights during the Soviet occupation of Estonia. The Institute of Historical Memory is a member of the Platform of European Memory and Conscience.
www.mnemosyne.ee

Unitas Foundation
The Unitas Foundation was established in 2008 with the mission to unite societies divided by totalitarian regimes. The organisation is based in Tallinn, but operates internationally. The Unitas Foundation is a member of the Platform of European Memory and Conscience.
www.unitasfoundation.org

The conference and its publication were made possible with the generous support of the Ministry of Education and Research, Open Estonia Foundation, and the Republic of Estonia Government Office.

Haridus- ja Teadusministeerium
Estonian Ministry of Education and Research

Avatud Eesti Fond
Open Estonia Foundation

Edited by Meelis Saueauk
Translation: Peeter Alan Tammisto, Aet Ringborg
Language editing: Refiner Translations OÜ
Layout: Aive Maasalu
Cover design: Kalle Paalits

ISBN 978-9949-32-617-4 (print)
ISBN 978-9949-32-649-5 (pdf)

University of Tartu Press
www.tyk.ee

Contents

Foreword

This collection consists of academic articles on the subjects addressed by the research conference "The Shaping of Identity and Personality under Communist Rule: History in the Service of Totalitarian Regimes in Eastern Europe," held at the Nordic Hotel Forum Conference Center in Tallinn, Estonia, on 9–10 June 2011 and arranged by the Estonian Institute of Historical Memory Foundation and the Unitas Foundation.

Identity as knowledge of oneself or self-identification in social circumstances and relations was something the Soviet-type communist countries in Central and Eastern Europe considered important to attempt to influence. This influence reached everyone and naturally gave rise to various sentiments and counter-reactions. The shaping of the identity "the new (Soviet) people" proved especially difficult in the countries and territories annexed by the Soviet Union during World War II (such as Estonia) or the Central and Eastern European countries subsumed into the Soviet bloc and Sovietized, where attempts were made to apply the same dogmas that had worked in Stalin's totalitarian USSR. To the former citizens of those previously more or less democratic countries, these attempts looked strange and absurd.

Ideologically mutated history was an important component of the official communist identity. The artificial official history and the new historical identity it forced upon the population aspired to establish the sole possible truth by means of half-truths, ignoring and suppressing events that had actually happened and people who had actually lived.

The organizers of the conference intended to describe, analyze, and explain the state policies and activities used in Eastern Europe for shaping the communist identity and personality by manipulating the historical consciousness, and the efficiency of those policies and activities, proceeding from the official historical approaches of the former Eastern bloc. As the identification of violations of human rights during the Soviet period is the principal mission of the Estonian Institute of Historical Memory, there was also research into connections between the restriction of human rights and the shaping of identity by force. A majority of the members of the Learned Committee of the Estonian Institute of Historical Memory were present at the conference, starting with Enrique Barón Crespo from Spain, lawyer and economist and former president of the European Parliament. Toomas Hendrik Ilves, president of the Republic of Estonia and patron of the Estonian Institute of Historical Memory, who gave a welcoming address at the conference, emphasized that we should not neglect the collection of local people's memories, oral history.

Probably the most important thread running through every article in this collection is the conflict between the official, communist identity and the nation's historical memory, and its consequences. For this collection, articles based on seven conference papers were selected.

All in all, the conference left us with hope that, even if it is difficult to assess the influence of propaganda and shaping the communist identity, the task is not impossible. And that identities are created more easily than they can be changed.

The organizers thank the Open Estonia Foundation and the Estonian Ministry of Education and Research, whose support has helped both the conference and this publication to become a reality.

Hopefully, the collection will provide fascinating and thought-provoking reading.

Meelis Saueauk
editor
Estonian Institute of Historical Memory

Introduction

Maria Mälksoo

The vulnerability of humans' sense of self against the totalitarian system has evoked the creative and inquisitive energies of writers, filmmakers, artists, and scholars alike. Arthur Koestler published his disillusioned critique of Soviet communism in 1940. The hero of his striking novel *Darkness at Noon* (1941) is unable to resist the Party's narrative, giving up on his sense of self and facing his execution convinced that he is serving the Revolution.[1] George Orwell's famous anti-totalitarian novel *Nineteen Eighty-Four* (1949) similarly sees the protagonist Winston Smith turned by the system so that he ends up loving "Big Brother." Still others, such as Czesław Miłosz, have pointed to the resilience of individuals in highly controlled societies in constructing their identities. In his *The Captive Mind* (1953), he describes the sizeable space for private discourse that existed in the Soviet bloc in parallel to the official narrative through the deceptive practice of Ketman. Nonetheless, his account is a poignant reminder of the moral difficulties one encounters while resisting the attempts of totalitarian and highly authoritarian systems to seek "enslavement through consciousness." In order to retain a sense of self, one generally reaches for memory, hoping to keep some sense of continuity of one's identity – and thus the struggle of man against power becomes, in Milan Kundera's (1980) shrewd observation, the "struggle of memory against forgetting."

This call has recently been taken up by a range of scholars from different disciplinary corners in order to examine the intertwined pasts and memory cultures of the states and societies of the former Soviet bloc. While the unwritten canon of the interdisciplinary field of memory studies has traditionally focused on the largely Western ways of remembrance and working through of the Western encounters with Nazism, the ongoing "Eastern European turn" in the explorations of the politics, idiosyncrasies, and functions of memory has considerably broadened the discipline's analytical

---

[1]   Koestler, A. *Darkness at Noon*. New York: Macmillan, 1941.

gaze. This is evidenced by works as varied as Catherine Merridale's *Night of Stone* (2000), Anne Applebaum's *Gulag* (2003), Orlando Figes's *The Whisperers* (2007), Harald Wydra's *Communism and the Emergence of Democracy* (2007), Irina Paperno's *Stories of the Soviet Experience* (2009), David Satter's *It Was a Long Time Ago and It Never Happened Anyway* (2012), a collaborative book *Remembering Katyn* (2012) put together by the Slavic studies scholars of the University of Cambridge,[2] and Alexander Etkind's *Warped Mourning* (2013). Yet as this list of titles demonstrates, the empirical emphasis of the recent book-length studies on the tense relationship between the attempted creation of a uniform communist identity and the historical memory of its manifold subjects has more often than not focused on the case of Russia, and occasionally Poland.

The present collection of conference papers is a refreshing addendum in that regard, as it embraces accounts ranging from various Eastern European countries (such as Romania, the former Yugoslavia, and Poland) to the Baltic states. While the former certainly pursued different trajectories and identity politics than the Soviet Union, the ideological underpinnings of these communist regimes, in spite of their varying intensity and national "ownership," make their analysis in a comparative framework nonetheless legitimate. Bringing together Estonian and Latvian encounters with the Soviet attempts to mold their national self-identifications and historical memories according to the official Party line of the USSR, and the respective processes in Soviet Union's Eastern European satellites, is further validated by the focus on the periods in Romania's, Slovenia's and Poland's communist pasts, which are comparable to the level of repression and ideological rigidity otherwise characteristic of the Soviet Union. The problem of comparing apples and oranges is thus considerably tempered. That being said, the volume hardly argues for the homogenization of the region either. It is important to note that the debate over the precise nature of the communist regimes in the Soviet Union and Eastern Europe goes a long way back and continues to this day. While the concept of totalitarianism has gone out of fashion due to its Cold War associations in scholarly literature,[3] Adam Michnik's declaration that "there is no such thing as non-totalitarian ruling communism. It either becomes totalitarian or it ceases to be communism"[4] still holds considerable

---

[2] See further: Project "Memory At War: Cultural Dynamics at Poland, Russia and Ukraine," www.memoryatwar.org.

[3] See also Lebow, R. *The Politics and Ethics of Identity: In Search of Ourselves*. Cambridge: Cambridge University Press, 2012, 5.

[4] Michnik, A. *Letters from Prison and Other Essays*. Berkeley and Los Angeles: University of California Press, 1985, 47.

appeal for those who actually lived under and directly experienced the daily realities of Soviet and Eastern European communist regimes. This is well reflected in the conceptual underpinnings of the authors of this volume as well.

While this collection of papers serves as yet another reminder of the inroads the "memory boom" has recently made in the countries of Central and Eastern Europe, it is by and large a compilation of historians' work. Not coincidentally, the papers substantiate the intricacies between the attempts to forge a uniform communist identity at the expense of national historical memories and self-identifications, rather than conceptually engage the relationship between identity and collective memory in its many disguises *per se*. The aim of this short introduction is thus to provide the volume with some conceptual center of gravity by shedding light on the notions of identity and historical memory, their complex relationship, and ethico-political implications.

Identity and memory

It has become a truism of social memory studies that memory and identity are intertwined and linked by mutually constitutive ties. If a commonsensical assumption serves right, "we are what we remember."[5] Anthony D. Smith has even put forth the argument "no memory, no identity; no identity, no nation."[6] Subsequently, the making and remaking of national, and increasingly also transnational, identities via the political use of memory has been the leitmotif of most of the literature on the relationship between memory and politics.[7] The political use of the past is hence hardly specific to totalitarian and authoritarian systems. However, their attempts to mold and manipulate the way people remember and relate to their pasts can be distinguished from

---

[5] Fentress, J., and Wickham, C. *Social Memory*. Oxford and Cambridge, MA: Blackwell, 1992, 7.

[6] Smith, A.D. Memory and Modernity: Reflections on Ernest Gellner's Theory of Nationalism. *Nations and Nationalism* 2, no. 3 (1996), 371–388, 383.

[7] Müller, J. W. (ed.). *Memory and Power in Post-War Europe: Studies in the Presence of the Past*. New York: Cambridge University Press, 2002; Olick, J. (ed.). *States of Memory: Continuities, Conflicts, and Transformations in National Perspective*. Durham, NC: Duke University Press, 2003; Lebow, R., Kansteiner, W., and Fogu, C. *The Politics of Memory in Postwar Europe*. Durham, NC: Duke University Press, 2006; Berger, T. *War, Guilt, and World Politics after World War II*. Cambridge: Cambridge University Press, 2012; cf. Bell, D. (ed.). *Memory, Trauma and World Politics: Reflections on the Relationship between Past and Present*. Palgrave Macmillan: Houndmills, Basingstoke, Hampshire, 2006.

less sinister ways of "engaging the public" by their level of repressiveness, utter denial of plurality, and the underlying belief in the possibility of remaking human nature. It was thus not so much the selection of those parts of the past that Nazis and communists wished to preserve that made their memory politics objectionable; it was more their assumption of the right to decide what would be available to others, as Tzvetan Todorov maintains.[8] A common method, as we also learn from these conference proceedings, was an attempt at organized forgetting.[9] Harald Wydra's description of this technique of imposing a "politically correct" line is worth quoting at length here:

> First, the destruction of memory aimed to invalidate any uncontrolled references to historical time before the advent of Soviet communism. Similarly, the claim to infallibility required constant adjustments of historical reality to the needs of communist parties. Second, totalitarian language came along with a "culture of lies" preventing groups with alternative visions about their identity from emerging. Organised forgetting was based on a tissue of lies, inventions, and fantasies that was unconsciously sustained by dissimulation and had a disastrous effect on group identity and historical consciousness. Finally, the public space was characterised by "communicative silencing," by a death of open historical debate, of critical discussion, and of exchange of memories to which the public acquiesced for fear of losing social opportunities and social mobility.[10]

It is indeed proof of the genius of Orwell, who famously captured the political importance of the past for totalitarian rulers through his dictum, "Who controls the past controls the future; who controls the present controls the past."

Nonetheless, a warning against the simplistic essentialization of "national historical memory" against equally reified "communist identity" is warranted. The relationship between memory and identity is hardly unequivocal, even in highly repressive regimes, as this collection of papers also evocatively demonstrates. The problems start with the shorthand term "collective memory," which implies a definitive homogeneity of views regarding the past. This, however, could not be further from the truth even in totalitarian societies, despite the state's various efforts to forge an official historical and

---

8   Todorov, T. *Hope and Memory: Reflections on the Twentieth Century*. London: Atlantic Books, 2003, 127.
9   Connerton, P. *How Societies Remember*. Cambridge: Cambridge University Press, 1989, 14–15.
10 Wydra, H. *Communism and the Emergence of Democracy*. Cambridge: Cambridge University Press, 2007, 228.

identitarian narrative through political rhetoric (including propaganda), commemoration, education (including history-writing), and punishment.[11] Historical memory does not directly mirror or represent the past under any circumstances, be they societally repressive or liberal. Indeed, it might be worthwhile to take our cue from Duncan S. Bell, who suggests distinguishing more clearly between social memory, mythology, and critical history. Even though offering yet another ideal-typical taxonomy (for these three forms of molding and reproducing national consciousness overlap and interpenetrate at various points in reality), this classification is helpful in distinguishing better between various forms of historical representation.[12]

Similar issues are raised by the widespread assumption that identities – individual and collective alike – are unique and consistent. As constructivist international-relations scholar Richard Ned Lebow argues in his recent book, there is "nothing inevitable about contemporary understandings of identity or their relative appeal."[13] The diversity of identity discourses and related political projects is arguably as varied within Western culture as the alleged differences between it and its non-Western counterparts. The communist utopia, and the accompanying modernist project of building a communist state in the Soviet Union and its outer satellites in Eastern Europe, tried to do away with interiority and reflexivity of human beings, as these were seen as sources of alienation and social and political unrest. The communist utopia thus operated with a thin description of identity which reduced human beings to bodies and minds that live entirely in the present. Accordingly, the communist systems sought to advance communal values and goals at the expense of suppressing individual autonomy and expressions, leading to "one of the most pessimistic conclusions of the twentieth century...[that is] the extent to which efforts to construct utopias are likely to produce dystopias."[14]

It is no wonder, then, that the collapse of the communist regimes in Soviet Union and Eastern Europe brought about a vigorous search to re-connect the fragmented memories in the endeavors to construct new – and occasionally resurrect old – (national) identities. Various measures and degrees of transitional justice were applied in order to delineate the contents of new political communities that had emerged from the socially traumatizing

---

[11] Berger, op. cit., 12.
[12] For a selection of classical and more recent classifications of collective memory, see the works of Durkheim, Halbwachs, Aleida Assmann, Jan Assmann, Olick and Wydra in the Selected Literature.
[13] Lebow, op. cit., 2–3.
[14] Ibid., 37, 42.

experience of communism.[15] Yet again, the role of memory for identity-building became highlighted in the process, even though it has generally been understood as an emotional source of healing and reconciliation rather than a technique of political engineering, possibly creating as many new lines of division as it hopes to resolve the old ones.

Touching upon the complex relationship between identity and memory in the context of public rituals, private communication, ideological pressure, propaganda, and transitional justice in various communist societies of the former Soviet Union and Eastern Europe, this volume reminds us of E.H. Carr's observation about the two-way traffic between past and present. This implies that the past can only be viewed and understood "through the eyes of the present,"[16] just as this collection of conference papers is a way to work through and relate critically to the difficult and multi-layered communist legacies in Eastern Europe in the country-specific post-communist/post-socialist contemporary contexts. It is up to the reader to decide to what extent the collected volume can be regarded as a scholarly venture contributing to the particular domestic struggles of identity-building, or rather a humble undertaking in critical history.

Guide to the papers

The opening paper of the volume, by **Silviu Taraş** (Babeş-Bolyai University, Romania), examines collective identity construction via the public rituals introduced by the Communist Party in postwar Romania (1944–1948). Through the example of Romania's Covasna County, which has a significant Hungarian population, Taraş discusses the ritualization of social relations at a critical moment of the rise and consolidation of the Communist Party's power as means of maintaining social control. Applying a discursive perspective, he demonstrates the competition between ritualized "political festivals," their suggested symbolic reality, and the subversive counter-images contesting the hegemonic representations in various ways. This paper thus refutes the assumption of identity construction in a communist system as the exclusive realm of social engineering.

---

[15] On transitional justice in the former communist bloc in general, see Stan, L. *Transitional Justice in Eastern Europe and the Former Soviet Union: Reckoning with the Communist Past. Abingdon, Oxon, and New York: Routledge, 2009*; and the Baltic states in particular, see the works of Eva-Clarita Onken (see also under Eva-Clarita Pettai) in the Selected Literature.

[16] Carr, E.H. *What is History?* Houndmills, Basingstoke, Hampshire: Palgrave, 2001, 19.

The contribution by **Eli Pilve** (University of Tartu, Estonia, and the Estonian Institute of Historical Memory) takes account of the practice of ideological pressure and indoctrination in the Soviet Estonian school system as part of the educational Sovietization of the country. Her analysis ranges from discussing the "communist component" of teaching history and literature as the most common sources of consciousness (be it ideological or national) and targets of ideological education thereof, to geography, foreign languages, music, art, and sciences across the whole Soviet period. As she shows, even though Stalin's death in 1953 and the subsequent denunciation of his cult of personality by Khrushchev had a palpable effect on the ideological atmosphere in Soviet Estonian schools, the personality cult of the leader merely gave way to a wider Party cult in historiography and teaching. Communist ideological pedagogy, therefore, largely remained intact throughout the Soviet period in Estonia. However, maintains Pilve, the pupils' "communist upbringing" did not reshape the Estonian civic identity as intended, but instead contributed to the emergence and reinforcement of their parallel consciousness.

The following papers by **Simo Mikkonen** (University of Jyväskylä, Finland), **Ivo Juurvee** (University of Tartu, Estonia), and **Maarja Talgre** (Swedish Radio) tackle the problem of Soviet historical propaganda vis-à-vis the Baltic emigrants from various scholarly and personal perspectives. Using archival materials from Tallinn and Moscow, Mikkonen's paper outlines the ways Soviet officials regarded and attempted to influence the Estonian émigrés' "hearts and minds" concerning their former homeland via manifold measures of soft power.

Ivo Juurvee concentrates on what is known as the "second wave" of the printed Soviet propaganda directed towards Estonians in the West, which began in 1958 with the establishment of the newspaper *Kodumaa* (*Homeland*). This publication was intended to be distributed among Estonians in the West on the initiative of the KGB (Committee for State Security of the Soviet Union). The article offers a vivid account of the role of one particular individual – Andrus Roolaht – behind these propaganda efforts. While *Kodumaa* sought to discredit the Estonian political leaders abroad, trying, and occasionally managing, to split the émigré community by creating discord among the diaspora, the KGB-generated publications nonetheless failed to leave their mark on the international English-language historiography. **Maarja Talgre**, a Swedish journalist of Estonian heritage, continues this thread with a powerful and painful personal account, reiterating the effects of encountering Soviet propaganda and the cynicism of Andrus Roolaht in person.

Jernej Letnar Černič (Graduate School of Government and European Studies, Slovenia) explores the remnants of communist identity in contemporary Slovenia, addressing the pitfalls and prospects of transitional justice towards communist crimes in the country. His account is strongly normative, arguing the need for a particular (i.e., legally framed) remembrance of the communist legacy in Slovenia.

KlintaLočmele (University of Latvia) applies a trauma theory-inspired perspective in analyzing the generational transmission of the Soviet experience and communication of the issues of the past in contemporary Latvian families. Drawing on sociological surveys conducted in six secondary schools in the Latgale region of Latvia, Ločmele shows that while the older members of Latvian families willingly discuss the everyday routine of the Soviet years with their children, they are rather passive in communicating the more serious events and processes that punctuated their lives under the Soviet regime (such as state violence and deportations).

The final paper of the volume, by **Agata Fijalkowski** (Lancaster University, UK), takes up the paradoxes of constructing a judicial identity in two critical periods of Polish history: the Stalinist era (1944–1956) and martial law (1981–1983). Importantly, she also demonstrates "the presence of the past" by observing the ways the (mal)administration of justice during these periods has resurfaced and been dealt with in post-1989 Poland. As she shows, efforts made by the judiciary to reassert itself as a profession after the Stalinist period only occurred after the retirement of the former cadre, reform of legal education, and development of civil society. Even during martial law, the courts sought to work around the draconian measures, and orders were not followed blindly. Her linking of the earlier debates with contemporary Polish discussions on the appropriate range of transitional justice measures provides a suitable endpoint to this volume, as it seeks to understand the remnants of the communist legacy in contemporary Eastern Europe.

Selected literature

Applebaum, Anne. *Gulag: A History.* New York: Doubleday, 2003.
Assmann, Aleida. *Erinnerungsräume: Formen und Wandlungen des kulturellen Gedächtnisses.* Munich: C.G. Beck, 2003.
Assmann, Aleida. Re-Framing Memory: Between Individual and Collective Forms of Constructing the Past. In *Performing the Past: Memory, History, and Identity in Modern Europe*, eds. Karin Tilmans, Frank van Vree, and Jay Winter. Amsterdam: Amsterdam University Press, 2010, 35–50.

Assmann, Jan. Collective Memory and Cultural Identity. *New German Critique* no. 65 (1995), 125–133.

Assmann, Jan. *Moses the Egyptian: The Memory of Egypt in Western Monotheism.* Cambridge, MA, and London: Harvard University Press, 1997.

Assmann, Jan. *Das kulturelle Gedächtnis: Schrift, Erinnerung und politische Identität in frühen Hochkulturen.* Munich: Beck, 1999.

Bell, Duncan S.A. Mythscapes: Memory, Mythology, and National Identity. *British Journal of Sociology* 54, no. 1 (2003), 63–81.

Bell, Duncan S.A., ed. *Memory, Trauma and World Politics. Reflections on the Relationship between Past and Present.* Palgrave Macmillan: Houndmills, Basingstoke, Hampshire, 2006.

Bell, Duncan S.A. Agonistic Democracy and the Politics of Memory. *Constellations: An International Journal of Critical and Democratic Theory* 15, no. 1 (2008), 148–166.

Berger, Thomas U. *War, Guilt, and World Politics After World War II.* Cambridge: Cambridge University Press, 2012.

Carr, E.H. *What is History?* Houndmills, Basingstoke, Hampshire: Palgrave, 2001.

Connerton, Paul. *How Societies Remember.* Cambridge: Cambridge University Press, 1989.

Durkheim, Émile. *The Elementary Forms of Religious Life.* New York: Free Press, 1995.

Etkind, Alexander, Rory Finnin, Uilleab Blacker, Julie Fedor, Simon Lewis, Maria Mälksoo, and Matilda Mroz. *Remembering Katyn.* Cambridge: Polity Press, 2012.

Etkind, Alexander. *Stories of the Undead in the Land of the Unburied.* Stanford: Stanford University Press, 2013.

Fentress, James, and Chic Wickham. *Social Memory.* Oxford and Cambridge, MA: Blackwell, 1992.

Figes, Orlando. *The Whisperers: Private Lives in Stalin's Russia.* New York: Picador, 2007.

Halbwachs, Maurice. *On Collective Memory.* Chicago: University of Chicago Press, 1992.

Halbwachs, Maurice. *Les cadres sociaux de la mémoire.* Paris: Albin Michel, 1994.

Koestler, Arthur. *Darkness at Noon.* New York: Macmillan, 1941.

Kundera, Milan. *The Book of Laughter and Forgetting.* New York: Alfred A. Knopf, 1980.

Lebow, Richard Ned, Wulf Kansteiner, and Claudio Fogu. *The Politics of Memory in Postwar Europe.* Durham, NC: Duke University Press, 2006.

Lebow, Richard Ned. *The Politics and Ethics of Identity: In Search of Ourselves.* Cambridge: Cambridge University Press, 2012.

Merridale, Catherine. *Night of Stone: Death and Memory in Twentieth Century Russia.* New York: Penguin, 2000.

Michnik, Adam. *Letters from Prison and Other Essays.* Berkeley and Los Angeles: University of California Press, 1985.

Miłosz, Czesław. *The Captive Mind.* New York: Vintage, 1990.

Müller, Jan-Werner, ed. *Memory and Power in Post-War Europe: Studies in the Presence of the Past.* New York: Cambridge University Press, 2002.

Olick, Jeffrey K. Collective Memory: The Two Cultures. *Sociological Theory* 17, no. 3 (1999), 333–348.

Olick, Jeffrey K., ed. *States of Memory: Continuities, Conflicts, and Transformations in National Perspective.* Durham, NC: Duke University Press, 2003.

Onken, Eva-Clarita. The Politics of Finding Historical Truth: Reviewing Baltic History Commissions and Their Work. *Journal of Baltic Studies* 39, no. 1 (2007), 109–116.

Orwell, George. *1984.* New York: Harcourt, Brace and Company, 1949.

Paperno, Irina. *Stories of the Soviet Experience: Memoirs, Diaries, Dreams.* Ithaca, NY: Cornell University Press, 2009.

Pettai, Eva-Clarita. "The Convergence of Two Worlds: Historians and Emerging Histories in the Baltic States." In *Forgotten Pages in Baltic History. Inclusion and Exclusion in History. A Festschrift for John Hiden*, eds. Martyn Housden and David J. Smith. Amsterdam and New York: Rodopi, 2011, 263–279.

Satter, David. *It Was a Long Time Ago, and It Never Happened Anyway: Russia and the Communist Past.* New Haven and London: Yale University Press, 2012.

Smith, Anthony D. Memory and Modernity: Reflections on Ernest Gellner's Theory of Nationalism. *Nations and Nationalism* 2, no. 3 (1996), 371–388.

Stan, Lavinia. *Transitional Justice in Eastern Europe and the Former Soviet Union: Reckoning with the Communist Past.* Abingdon, Oxon, and New York: Routledge, 2009.

Todorov, Tzvetan. *Hope and Memory: Reflections on the Twentieth Century.* London: Atlantic Books, 2003.

Wydra, Harald. *Communism and the Emergence of Democracy.* Cambridge: Cambridge University Press, 2007.

Public Rituals in Transformation – Identity Politics in Communist Romania

Silviu Taraş

The construction of a new collective identity in postwar Romania was a complex process of integrating "progressive traditions" without leaving the narrow path of ideological assumptions, dealing with the influence of the Church without alienating the masses, and proclaiming national equality in regions where in the recent past the struggle between majority and minority ethnic groups caused wounds that had yet to heal. The ambitious agenda to alter the foundations of social existence and ultimately to create the "New Man" made communists the catalysts of social structure and thus separated "Them" from the rest of society.

The paper is constructed on a chronological overview of the different images of "the Other" and an analysis of the Romanian communist regime's restructuring of public space and collective identity, preceded by conceptual clarifications. We argue that the projection of effective images of the Other, and the integration of the reinterpreted past, were two main features of the identity politics of the Janus-faced Romanian communist regime.

The idiosyncratic nature of the Eastern European communist regimes makes inadequate the matrix of analysis employed in the study of ceremonies in Western societies. Therefore, the theoretical introduction to the study of public rituals and identity politics encounters the need for conceptualization, a transformation of the almost "colligatory concepts" in useful analytic rubrics. The present paper refrains from a detailed presentation of the debates in the literature on these concepts. Instead, this paper is situated in the field of relevant scholarship according to the following vectors and basic assumptions of interpretation.

In their efforts to mold public opinion, the communist parties used *cumulative* rather than selective legitimation. They did not choose between intellectual and emotional communication, between reformist continuity and revolutionary breaks, or between traditional, charismatic, and rational authority; they covered the whole spectrum. Therefore, the systemic shift between the "invented tradition" of Marxist language and the existing sets of social imagination did not produce so categorically, as seemed on a superficial plane. Moreover, in the case of Romania, in the confrontation between the two sets of idioms the Party considered persuasive – the Marxist discourse and the language of national values – the latter gradually displaced the former.[1] Consequently, the conceptual point of departure regarding the proposed discussion of identity, legitimacy, and ideology is a *discursive* perspective, emphasizing the linkage between legitimacy and ideology(ies), as well as the immanent presence of this discourse in the public rituals. The word "ideology" has a whole range of useful meanings, not all of which are compatible with each other or applicable to the paper's topic. Therefore it is necessary to articulate the understanding of the concept as it will be used in the following. For this purpose we will define the normative and epistemological aspect of the term and its relation with legitimacy.

The means of achieving political legitimacy by constructing a new collective identity is considered a marginal issue in the history of the communist regimes. Even though the symbolic means of securing citizens' adherence to the dominant system of signifying practices were not dominant, it was part of the structural totality of legitimizing acts. Legitimacy and collective identity, in the sense implied here, largely follows the conceptual frame set by the redefinition of the term by Katherine Verdery, "the nonorganization of an effective counterimage."[2] It presupposes not the consent of the whole population but the assent of part of the population and the lack of an alternative image of social organization. Even if we were in a position to do so, it would not be our task, for the purpose we have in mind, to give a thorough analysis of the different meanings of "legitimacy." Instead, given the intertwined character of legitimacy and commemorative ceremonials and rituals, in the following section these will be discussed as parts of a structured totality of one phenomenon.

Christel Lane, presenting a historical account of the Soviet mass political holiday, argues that the role of these ceremonies is, among other things, the strengthening and justifying of the present by reference to the past.[3] The character of these rites is "commemorative" and *re-enacts* the past in the sense of changing the ontological status of had-been-ness into a meta-

---

[1] Verdery, K. *National Ideology under Socialism: Identity and Cultural Politics in Ceauşescu's Romania.* Berkeley, Los Angeles, and London: University of California Press, 1995, 9.

[2] Verdery, op.cit., 10.

[3] Lane, C. *The Rites of Rulers.* Cambridge: Cambridge University Press, 1981, 153.

physical present. Paul Connerton implies this meaning of the ritual function of commemorative ceremonies by assessing the legitimating role of past images for the existing social order.[4] The discussion of the role and function of the commemorative ceremonies raises the taxonomic problem of conceptualization of the terms "ceremony," "ritual," and "holiday." From a functionalist and structuralist point of view, differences were signaled between ritual and ceremony. According to the functionalist approach, ceremony is secular, and ritual is a religious activity. According to the structuralist view, ritual is the highly formalized act of symbolic means, while ceremony connotes more flexibility and spontaneity.[5] Given that the goal of the present inquiry is not the elaboration of a generic analytical rubric of rituals, but the analysis of identity politics, this distinction will be abandoned. From Mona Ozouf's thorough analysis of the festivals of the French Revolution, certain aspects regarding the nature, function, and role of the ceremonials are relevant to the discussion of the public festivals of the communist regimes.[6]

The first of the problems considers the consubstantiality between the content and form of the ceremonies and the political and social context of their occurrence. In this perspective it would be possible to categorize the ceremonials according to the various political intentions that motivated them. This raises the broad problem of to what extent the political mass rituals are manifestations of political power, and the question of the "invented traditions" of the ceremonies. Some research, primarily sociological in inspiration, centers on the functional relationship between power and ceremonial.[7] Is the spectacle and ritual of the ceremonials the handmaiden of power? Do such ceremonials reinforce community, or hierarchy, or both? David Cannadine argues that the spectacle and pageantry of the ceremonials are an integral part of the power and politics themselves. Moreover, he asserts that "ritual is not a mask of force, but is itself a type of power."[8] This *integralist* approach of the ritual and ceremonial in modern political culture, which considers rituals

---

4   Connerton, P. *How Societies Remember.* Cambridge: Cambridge University Press, 1989, 3.

5   For the details of these differences, see Leach, E. *Culture and Communication: The Logic by which Symbols are Connected;An Introduction to the Use of Structuralist Analysis in Social Anthropology.* Cambridge: Cambridge University Press, 1993; and Turner, V.W. *The Ritual Process: Structure and Anti-Structure.* Ithaca, NY: Cornell University Press, 1991.

6   Ozouf, M. *Festivals and the French Revolution.* Cambridge and London: Harvard University Press, 1988.

7   Cannadine, D., and Price S. (eds.). *Rituals of Royalty: Power and Ceremonial in Traditional Societies.* Cambridge: Cambridge University Press, 1987, 4.

8   Ibid., 19.

neither the exercise of power nor the practice of politics by other, subsidiary transient means, is reinforced by David Kertzer in his book *Ritual, Politics and Power.*[9] Kertzer, in his analysis of the symbolism of politics, asserts that "[…] ritual is an integral part of politics in modern industrial societies."[10] This approach, congruent with the one suggested by Mona Ozouf and Christel Lane, considers ceremonies and rituals instruments of *doing* politics by symbolic means. The highly formalized character of the rituals brings into question the attribution of a strange omnipotence to the organizer's projects and explains the relative stability of the forms of celebration over a wide historical span. Therefore, the reading of the web of quasi-textual symbols of the communist ceremonies encounters the deficiency of making unmediated and direct connections between the form and content of the mass political rituals and its context. However, in these deliberately engineered rituals, the meaning accorded them by the organizers triumphed in certain perspectives over the aforementioned inherent conservative character of the ritual form. For example, the emergence of Nicolae Ceausescu's cult of personality can be directly correlated with the decreasing number of high officials on the official tribune during the ceremony.

PARADA MILITARĂ ŞI DEMONSTRAŢIA OAMENILOR MUNCII DIN CAPITALĂ

23 August 1965. The official tribune representing the "collective leadership"

---

9   Kertzer, D. *Ritual, Politics and Power.* London: Yale University Press, 1988.
10   Ibid., 3.

23 August 1985. The "Leader" and the "Scientist" – Nicolae and Elena Ceausescu

Nevertheless, the interpretation of the communist ceremonials has to be aware of the difference between this careful assumption and the misleading view of the ceremonial as docile machinery to be set up or taken down at a stroke, according to the needs of the cause. Congruent with Mona Ozouf's idea that "although the legislator makes the laws for the people, festivals make the people for the laws,"[11] a case for seeing ceremonials as an indispensable complement to the legislative system can be made in the case of the communist ceremonials as well.

The intentionality of the public festivals to create legitimacy, to mold collective identity, and to control society through symbolic means implies the role of the "political pedagogy" of these rituals. I. Timoshin, a Soviet writer on the subject of mass political holidays, outlines four basic roles that the revolutionary political holidays have performed over the years:[12] the ritual is supposed to "remind the working class of its victories and to honor the heroes of revolutionary events," to create unity and solidarity among the workers, and "to demonstrate the successes and achievements of the new generation." Finally, the ritual is supposed to express a special kind of *communion*, that involves "the demonstration of unity of purpose of the people, the Party and the State; it is a demonstration of love of the Motherland, the social system, and the ideas of communism."[13] According to Hobsbawm, the need for the invention of traditions arose in the new context of nineteenth-century

---

[11]   Ozouf, op. cit., 9.
[12]   Timoshin, quoted by Christel Lane, op. cit., 153.
[13]   Ibid., 154.

politics, when politics as such was essentially becoming nationwide politics.[14] In this sense the State, Nation, and Society converged, and the State faced unprecedented problems of how to maintain or even establish the obedience, loyalty, and cooperation of its subjects or members – in other words, its own legitimacy. Without overemphasizing the role of "invented traditions" in the analysis of the communist mass political celebrations, there are certain aspects to be considered. Hobsbawm defines the invention of tradition as a process "of formalization and ritualization, characterized by reference to the past, if only by imposing repetition."[15] This implies a legitimating process with reference to the past, generally a constructed one, with which a historical continuity is created by semi-fiction or simply historical forgery. The imaginative persuasiveness of the re-enactment of the past event was worked out by employing a calendrically observed articulation.

The very distinctive feature of the commemorative ceremonials, which differentiates them from the more general category of rituals, is that they not only imply continuity with the past but also explicitly claim such continuity. Consequently, rites of this sort possess a distinctive characteristic that can be described as *re-enactment*. The re-enactment of a past event infers the suppression of the temporal distance between past and present, and by doing that the reality of the present is re-evaluated, covered, or even rejected. The materiality of the textual or quasi-textual symbols ceases to be a mere "reflection" of the past and becomes presence. Because this intended consequence is meant to be produced in the consciousness of the participants, it goes beyond the scope of the present inquiry, but it also draws the attention on the participants of the ceremonial.

The importance of popular resonance is asserted by Paul Connerton: "people resist to pay lip-service to an alien set of rites, [...] because to enact a rite is always, in some sense, to assent to its meaning."[16] The presupposed voluntary participation in the public festivals sheds light on the other function performed by communist rituals, the insurance of *social control*. In pre-revolutionary France, the *ancien regime* considered the ceremonials "safety valves": the authorized excesses were channeled and thus stopped from spreading into daily life.[17] In the case of the communist ceremonials, the participation of the masses in the rites ensured a certain level of assent for the

---

[14] Hobsbawm, E. Mass-Producing Traditions: Europe, 1870–1914. In Hobsbawm, E., and Rangers, T. (ed.). *The Invention of Tradition*. Cambridge: Cambridge University Press, 1983, 264.
[15] Hosbawm, E. Introduction: Inventing Traditions. In *The Invention of Tradition*, 4.
[16] Connerton, op. cit., 64.
[17] Ozouf, op. cit., 4.

political elite. Because of the restricted character of the ritual acts, posture and language infer explicitness; the ritual communication is, to a certain degree, cleared of the hermeneutic puzzles. One gives the salute of the Communist Youth, or one does not; it is a display of an explicit statement. Even if this bodily communication had no correspondence in one's consciousness, performing the appropriate gestures and speech acts meant a degree of assent.

There is a general inclination in the assumptions about the revolutionary changes, asserted both by its actors and posterity, to consider them the moment of the end of the preceding historical period and the beginning of something new and different. This view of a radical break with the past, claimed especially in regard to the French Revolution and the communist seizure of power, has been challenged. Under the veil of the radical changes introduced by those who claimed the break with the past, certain elements survived the purge and were consciously or unconsciously used thereafter. Accordingly, the appealing view of *invented tradition* regarding the communist commemorative ceremonials has to be used with caution. Richard Stites, in his study of the origins of Soviet ritual style, showed the double character of these rituals: "[the commemorative ceremony of] November 7 was a complex blend of carnival, monument, rhetoric, and sacrality which together offered a picture of continuity and change, of mystery and majesty."[18] This feature of the communist political ritual from an epistemological point of view is the cognitive/affective content. The public side of the ceremonial consists of a complex set of activities in which ritual is intermingled with dramatic and political activities and decorative-political art so that the boundaries between the various types of activity become fuzzy. On the one hand, considered as a means of political pedagogy, the ritual of commemorative ceremonial as quasi-textual representation in symbolic form possesses cognitive content. On the other hand, the form of the ritual, the spectacle and pageantry aims for the subconscious assent of the participants. This duplicity resembles Turkish philosopher Abu Nasr al-Farabi's vision of the Virtuous City. In this city "there are two classes of citizens: the wise men who are able to cognize God, incorporeal realities, and the nature of human happiness; and those who are able to know these things only through images. [...] It is the duty of the wise men to instruct the common people and provide them with appropriate images concerning the reality of things."[19]

---

[18] Stites, R. The Origins of Soviet Ritual Style: Symbol and Festival in the Russian Revolution. In Arvidsson, C., and Blomquist, L.E. (eds.). *Symbols of Power.* Stockholm: Almquist & Wiksell, 1987, 40.

[19] Traschys, op. cit., 173.

Because the political elite in the communist regime was highly committed to the achievement of value consensus, that is, the perception of social reality shared by the leaders and the led, they had to choose among three strategies.[20] The first strategy would infer the change of the social conditions in order to bring them closer to the ideological definition. Second, they could change the consciousness of the ruled to bring the perception of the social reality closer to the ideological definition, or third, they could maintain social control by influencing the ruled to accept the discrepancy between the ideological definition and the reality of social relations. The ritual as instrument used by the political elite to gain acceptance of the general system of norms and values, and therefore as an instrument of cultural management, is at the same time a means to construct identity. The rituals in general and commemorative ceremonies in particular were one of the possible modalities to bridge the discrepancy between ideology and reality.

The calendar system of public festivals was regulated by the teleology promoted by the Party, and the canonical form of the number, sequence, and performative structure of these celebrations recovered the totality of the past. The ritual re-enactment of the past had a twofold consistency. On the one hand, through the inherent backward-looking character of commemoration, continuity was established with the past. On the other hand, through the repetitiveness of the ritual, the transfigured reality of the past became a metaphysical present. The interpretation is grounded on the assumption that rituals have changed in their meaning over the span of time. Therefore, a better understanding of the rite is possible by situating it in the historical context, not only by *reading* additional information but by expanding the interpretation field from the ritual as a self-contained text and analyzing it with the theoretical and methodological tools of hermeneutic historicism.

Images of the Other – sources of the Self

Theoretical reflections centered on the relation between the Self and the Other consider this nexus in terms of boundary markers of identity. Moreover, the analyses performed by Dejan Jovic on the construction of the political frontier between the "Us" and "Others" by the communist Yugoslav political elite shows the *ab ovo* negative construction of the Self.[21] Thus, studying the

---

[20] Lane, op. cit., 27.
[21] Jovic, D. Communist Yugoslavia and Its "Others." In Lampe, J.R., and Mazower, M. *Ideology and National Identity in the 20th Century Southeastern Europe* (book manuscript submitted to the CEU Press in September 2002), 296–322.

Self/Other nexus, the starting point for Dejan Jovic was the identification of the identity construction in postwar Yugoslavia *in opposition* to its Others. Ivor B. Neumann asserts that the history of thinking about Self and Other stretches back to the Roman idea of persona, and since then it is argued that it has been a central theme of the Western philosophical reflection.[22] Hegel relates the identity formation to the Self/Other dichotomy and makes the inner connection of perceiving the Self in knowing the Other. This dialectical principle of identity formation was reformulated by Marx and became one of the dominant twentieth-century social theories.[23] Tzvetan Todorov considers the mediation as knowing a four-phase process.[24] He argues that the hermeneutic process of knowing divided in the four phases is a gradual progression toward an ideal and is a constant movement between the Self and the Other. The first phase of assimilating the Other to oneself is followed by the identification with it as the object of knowledge in the second phase. The dialogue between the Self and the Other is possible in the superior third phase, culminating in the knowing of the Other without maintaining one's own identity. This process of knowing determines one's perception of oneself in the same degree. The issue of identity formation in social theory took four paths: the ethnographic path, the psychological path, the Continental philosophical path, and the "Eastern excursion."[25] The presentation of these theoretical approaches is not central to the paper, and to avoid a taxonomical muddle, the paper proceeds to shape the discursive field in which the social image of the Other is articulated.

The locus of the discourse about identity in the communist period in Romania is defined to a high degree by its ideological vectors. However, before discussing the nature of the ideologically determined discourse, there are two important precursors. First, even if the term "Other(s)" is used for analytical purposes, entering the political and public discursive field means, at the same time, the displacement from the individual toward the collective level of identity and its counter-images. Second, in the socialist ideocratic system, the discursive field tended to be dominated by a single ideology. Katherine Verdery frames the analysis of the identity and cultural politics in Ceausescu's Romania by considering the discursive field of identity construction as dominated by the struggle between competing images of the

---

[22]   Neumann, I.B. *Uses of the Other: The East in European Identity Formation.* Minneapolis: University of Minnesota Press, 1999, 3.

[23]   Ibid., 4.

[24]   Todorov, T. *The Morals of History.* Minneapolis: University of Minnesota Press, 1995, 14.

[25]   Neumann, op. cit., 4.

Self.[26] She argues that in the case of Romanian communism, this was shaped by two powerful discourses: Marxism and the discourse on the nation. In this struggle, the discourse on the nation was capable of subordinating Marxism and subverting its terms.[27] The outcome of this encounter is coined in the literature as Romanian national-communism.

Before briefly sketching out the evolution of Romanian communism in order to argue the alternate feature of the Other in the case of Romanian communism, in accordance with the frame mapped out in the previous paragraphs, we should address one important conceptual difference between Katherine Verdery's and Dejan Jovic's analytical instrumentalization. Katherine Verdery discusses national ideology as constructed by the struggle of discourses that occurred in the "space of legitimation" with the participation of the intellectuals and not only the *ideologues* of the Party.[28] This is the premise of her conclusion that the national ideology somehow *forced* the communist leaders to adopt this "language." Dejan Jovic argues for the construction of the Yugoslav identity by the Party elite vision, in particularly emphasizing the role of Edvard Kardelj as an official and highly influential ideologue.[29]

For the understanding of the alternate feature of the image of the Other in the case of Romanian communism the – howsoever simplified – overview of the ideological changes is essential. In the succession of the different phases, quite arbitrarily separated, it is often argued that the developments in Romania were not synchronous with the political and ideological changes in the Soviet Union and other Eastern European countries. The overthrow of the king and the proclamation of the socialist state was followed by the first years of consolidation of the new regime, which was not Stalinist. Illustrated by the adoption of a pure Stalinist constitution in 1952, at a time when, all over the communist bloc, the process of de-Stalinization was starting, the discourse by the Party elite started to have accentuated Stalinist characteristics. Some researchers argue that real de-Stalinization never occurred in Romania,[30] which meant that the regime grew ossified. After a period of relaxation, and especially after Soviet troops withdrew from Romania (May 1958), new

---

[26] Verdery, K. *National Identity Under Socialism: Identity and Cultural Politics in Ceausescu's Romania.* Berkeley, Los Angeles, and London: University of California Press, 1995, 11.

[27] Ibid., 12.

[28] Ibid. 1–23, passim.

[29] Jovic, op.cit., 316–317.

[30] Schafir, M. *Romania: Politics, Economics and Society.* Boulder, CO: Lynne Rienner Publishers, 1985, 32–45; Campeanu, P. *Ceausescu, anii numaratorii inverse.* Bucharest: Editura Polirom, 2002, 143–247 ff.

elements gradually appeared in the official discourse that signaled a distancing from the Soviet Union in foreign policy, as well as a stronger presence of the discourse on the nation. This tendency culminated in the proclamations of Party autonomy from 1964 and the heyday of the Ceausescu regime: the proclamation in 1968 of noninterference in the domestic politics of the socialist countries. A new phase of the regime is generally considered to have started after the Ceausescus visited China and North Korea (1971). The "cultural revolution" proclaimed by the "July thesis" of 1971 (re)introduced the principle of the cult of personality. The 1980s, known as the "Golden Age" of the Romanian dynastic communism (more than 200 relatives of the "Family" were present in the various organizational levels of the Party and state), are characterized as a unique combination of communism and nationalism. As will be shown, the identification of the Other is more complex and problematic in the case of the Romanian communist regime because of the significant changes that took place.

Dejan Jovic deconstructs the temporality of the "original interpretation of the Marxist vision" of Yugoslav identity, showing the normative value of the analysis.[31] The enlightened vanguard's legitimizing vision of the future as the age of the achievement of the goals of the communist utopia has no Others. The socialist revolution as the final break with the "dark forces of the past" made the representation of it constitute an Other. "The past was described as a period of darkness replete with inequality, lack of freedom and injustice."[32] The reality of the present is the field of confrontation between the mentioned forces of the past and the progressive forces of socialist change. Communist political theory and social practice neglected the representation of reality as irrelevant. This is what every revolutionary regime starting with the French Revolution has done, as Francois Furet has eloquently shown.[33] In the process of constant change, the reality of the present becomes fluid and without significant relevance.

The common counter-image of the communist identity-constructing discourse was that of the "fascists." The legitimacy of existence and the leading role in society was essentially based in the late 1940s and maintained throughout the rule of the communist regimes on the "myth of liberation" of the country from the fascist yoke. The important legitimating force of the struggle against fascism is shown by the institution of the national holiday

---

[31] Jovic, op. cit., 297–300.
[32] Ibid., 298.
[33] Furet, F. *Interpreting the French Revolution*. Cambridge: Cambridge University Press, 1990, 55–59.

on 23 August, when "the Romanian people began the armed uprising, […] until finally German occupiers and their quisling tools were expelled from the country."[34] The role played in the event by the Red Army brings into discussion the process of the relationship between Romania and the Soviet Union as the external image of the Other.

The question of how the small and insignificant RCP could lead the struggle against fascism had to be answered. The first part of this was dealing with the leadership's esoteric knowledge of Marxism-Leninism, which they apparently thought granted them a clear insight and a consciousness that transcended that of ordinary humans. The second part of the answer had to deal with the Soviet Army's role in the event. Throughout the 1950s the role which the RCP claimed for itself in the liberation was *symbiotic*, not a substitution for that ascribed to the Soviet Union. This item was publicly reiterated with the occasion of the yearly celebration of the national holiday. The previously mentioned rift produced with the Soviet Union was followed by the total revision of the war historiography. The main element of this revision was the mentioning of the Soviet ultimatum, and by this the legitimation of the attack against the Soviet Union.[35] Parallel with the gradual detachment from the Soviets that culminated in the "moment of glory" of the Ceausescu regime, the 1968 proclamation of noninterference altered the hegemonic image of the "elder brother," the Soviet Union. This split in the communist camp was welcomed both by those communist regimes that also refused to accept "the leading role" of the Soviet Union and by the West. The former's opinion was bluntly expressed in the telegrams sent on the occasion of the Romanian national holiday. For instance, China's message in 1972 notes the "resolute opposition of the Romanians to interference, *hegemony*, and power politics […]."[36] The West's response to the Romanian political regime's "courageous" deed was symbolized by the visit of Western high officials (such as President Richard Nixon) and concretized by financial credits and political support. The relatively short period of good relations with the Western liberal-democratic systems produced a redefinition of the West as the Other. However, the change of the vectors in the discursive field was not so significant as in the case of the Soviets. Similarly to the Yugoslav case, the image of the West as a potential threat was never so important as in the case of the Soviet Union.

---

[34] HU OSA 300-60-1-612. Monitoring Romania, 554.
[35] Schafir, op.cit., 36.
[36] HU OSA 300-60-1-613, Romania Monitoring Agerpress, 549.

The first intra-systemic[37] Others as left deviations from the "indigenous interpretation of Marxism" were identified as the "Muscovites" of the RCP. This group, led by Ana Pauker and Vasile Luca, was associated with the Soviet implementation of the hegemonic policy and was convicted in a public trial in 1952.[38] The "dogmatists" as well as the "Stalinists" were another counter-image of the regime in Romania. In contrast with Yugoslavia, the dogmatists who were later identified with, for example, the *proletcultists* in the domain of cultural production occupied the leading positions in the 1950s. With the subsequent re-evaluation of the values, mainly on a national basis, those promoting Russian influence in literature and art were replaced. The bourgeois-nationalist intellectuals were purged from the institution in the 1950s, and later, alongside the adoption of an accentuated national language, the new turn produced and the national values were re-evaluated and reintroduced in the public sphere.

The illustrious case of right-wing deviation – the Patrascanu case (1954) – constituted the other important trial of the 1950s.[39] This trial was part of the internal struggle for power in the RCP as well as the "Muscovites" trial in the framework of the general purge of the communist parties in the socialist bloc. Patrascanu delivered a nationalistic speech in 1944 in Cluj (Transylvania), and this speech, along with other evidence of nationalism, was enough to get him sentenced to death. After the increased influence of the discourse on the nation and in a need for intra-systemic legitimacy Patrascanu was rehabilitated in 1965. As a side effect of this revival of the national values, the discourse against the Hungarian minority from Romania increased.

In the 1970s and 1980s, a new element in the idea of Romanian communist identity was introduced. As Andrei Brezianu pointed out, "the regime set forth the idea that being a Romanian and a communist was one and the same thing."[40] As a tool to create political legitimacy, Ceausescu exploited Romanian-Hungarian ethnic frictions and intensified appeals to chauvinistic sentiment. This is well illustrated by the 1982 appearance of a tract expounding the cultural superiority of Romanians over Hungarians, and the Political Press's publication two years later of *Elucidation of Facts (Fapte din umbra)*, which portrayed the Hungarians as a threat to world peace and stability.[41]

---

37 Schafir, op.cit., 48.
38 Campeanu, op. cit., 167.
39 Ibid., 195–234.
40 Finn, J. (ed.). *Romania: A Case of "Dynastic" Communism*. New York: Freedom House, 1989, 8.
41 Lacrajan, I. *Cuvant des pe Transilvania* [A Word about Transylvania]. Bucharest: Editura Politica, 1982.

Identity construction – the first years

In light of the aforementioned dynamic vectors that shaped identity in Romanian communism, in the following the analysis will be deepened by an attempt to capture the process of identity construction *in the making*. Communist parties used the ritualization of social relations as a means of maintaining social control; therefore public rituals became the *loci* of identity construction. The construction, enforcement, and consolidation of the new regime's festival calendar was a dynamic process bearing multiple influences. The concept of "political festival" is used in the following as an official anniversary or commemorative moment that entails several aspects: commemoration (of events or heroes), celebration (rites and their meaning), and informal holiday. In the period of ideological competition and the rise of the Communist Party, in Covasna County the time of the citizens was structured by four calendars in four different dimensions. In chronological order of their appearance, the first is the Christian calendar of the holy days, with slight differences among the existing four denominations. The second is the calendar of the Hungarian national holidays, concentrated around two major reference points of the nation's history: the 1848 Revolution and the founding of the Hungarian state by Saint Stephen. The third calendar, that of the democratic Romanian state, was set up immediately after World War I by the prefect's decree. This calendar also had two major thematic center points: the monarchy and the state. The fourth calendar is a structuring of the everyday life by the regime´s Power from three semantic fields: (1) international holidays, (2) commemorative festivals of the Soviet regime, and (3) the commemorative festivals of recent events of the new political regime *in statu nascendi*. The abundance of holidays and festivals is characteristic of the period of power transition. In order to create, consolidate, and reinforce the legitimacy of the ruling ideological discursive forces and the building of the new identity, the communists, in their pursuit of total control over society and the individual, transformed public festivals into symbolic dimensions of conflicting forces. The aim of this paper is not to propose the holistic description of the festival manifestations. It is instead to address public political rituals following the logics of three-dimensionality of the festivals (content, manifestation, and symbols) in order to shed light on the aspects of identity management by molding collective mentalities in the proposed time and space frame. Therefore, the interpretative paradigm defines the following structure of the paper. The systemic frame of interpretation is constructed on the typology of calendars and the three-dimensionality of festivals.

The national dimension cannot be reduced to the celebration of different holidays of the Hungarian calendar, such as the celebration of 15 March, as reference to the national symbols were present also in the pageantry and symbolism of the international, communist, and Soviet festivals. The issue of nationalism was addressed either explicitly by the speakers and symbols, or implicitly during the logistical problems raised and, last but not least, by the question of the reception. The ethnic structure of the county for the given period is an argument for the inevitability of national challenge. According to the 1930 census, out of the county's 136,122 inhabitants, there were 16,748 (12 percent) Romanians and 117,868 (86.6 percent) Hungarians.[42]

The emergence of Greater Romania after World War I brought an existential change in the lives of the Hungarians in Transylvania: they became a national minority. The burden of this status is suggested by the general excitement that preceded the entrance of the Hungarian army in Northern Transylvania in 1940. The festivities surrounding the army's entrance to cities and villages were thoroughly organized, and the reassertion of Hungarian authority in Northern Transylvania was overwhelmingly ritualized. By extending it to the whole territory and homogenizing the public rite, the image was created of belonging to a greater unity, inherently national and perceivable by the exteriorization of this essentially abstract entity. Thus territory became a concept subordinated to the "nation," and the new governors were aware of the social power that festivals and public rituals bring into being. One of the central rituals was the erection of a flagpole in every locality and the flying of the national flag there during the army parade. The importance of the discourse on the nation was amplified by the atrocities perpetrated in the proximity of authority transfers in 1940 and 1944, which amplified the tensions regarding the national issue.

This tension was also stimulated by the creation of two camps that held those accused of acts against the Romanians during the 1940–1944 period. One of the camps was established right next to the main city of the county, Sfântu Gheorghe, and held mainly Hungarians who fled with the retreating German and Hungarian army and came back in 1945. The significant number of prisoners in Feldioara camp and the harsh conditions of detention there alarmed the local community.[43] Illustrative for the interpretation field of

---

[42] *Recensământul General al Populației României din 29 decembrie 1930 [The Census of Romania's Population at December 29 1930] vol. II: Neam, limbă maternă, religie.* Bucharest: Ed. Monitorul Oficial, Imprimeria Națională, 1938, LX.

[43] See the issues of *Szabadság [Liberty]* newspaper from 1945.

national discourse after the re-entry of the Romanian authorities is the case of Private Sandu Dumitru.[44]

Festivals from this period present continuity and discontinuity alike. The authorities, in their pursuit of changing the topic of festivals and creating new boundaries between Us and Others, operated omissions, deliberately alternated the signifier of existing festivals, and invented new contents by imposing brand new public rituals. One of the most important new features in the content of the festival was its reference to a new set of values and norms brought by the dominant ideologică discourse. The ability of festivals to amplify and at the same time to quash time can be observed from two distinct perspectives. On the *vertical*, the commemorated event establishes a restrictive paradigm over the past, creating continuity and causality between events that occurred with substantial time span between them, overwhelming alternative interpretations by the logic of a Great Narrative. And on the *horizontal*, by covering the entire calendar cycle, a narrative is constructed that overlooks the possible festival days that do not harmonize with the imposed history course.

The interpretative paradigm of the festivals from 1944 to 1948 is, on the one hand, the teleology of a history of cooperation and brotherhood between Hungarians and Romanians, and between Hungarians and Russians, and on the other hand, of confrontations between Hungarians and Germans.[45] This interpretation cannot be overlooked in the analysis of commemorative public rituals of the 1848 Revolution and of the events additional to it. The vulgar-Marxist method of interpretation, theorized later by Bányai, is of course very simple and is structured in three different parts, in the order of their frequency: (1) the shared destiny of Hungarians and Romanians, (2) the history of conflicts between Hungarians and Germans, and (3) the shared history with Russians. The generic topic of cooperation with the Russian people encountered some difficulties; the key moment was "found" in the martyrdom of Russian officers who refused to fight against the Hungarian Revolution in 1848. This moment was exploited not only as the keystone of friendship between the two nations but also as the basis for the myth of

---

[44] This Romanian Army soldier was accused of participating in the murders in Aita Seacă village and was twice brought in front of villagers, who confirmed his innocence. ANJC [The National Archives of Covasna County], Comitetul Judeţean PCR Covasna, Fond 562, dosar nr.1/1945, f.44.

[45] For a detailed presentation, see Calendarul UPM, 1946, Ed. Falvak Nepe, Cluj, 1946; and another book by the same author: Bányai, L. *Közös sors – testvéri hagyományok [Common fate – brotherly traditions]*. Bucharest: Ed. Politică, 1973.

Russians' deep democratic character, as well as an example of the worldwide cooperation of imperialism.[46]

The deliberate alternation of the signifier was another procedure of misappropriation of an already institutionalized ritual with popular resonance. Portraying the new mother in an article of the local newspaper *Szabadság* (*Liberty*) is just another application of the logic of revolutionary antagonism: *until now* there were women sitting all day in coffee shops and pubs, but *from now on* the new society has other expectations.[47] The dualism of old and new sends us to another mythos of the period: the utopia of new beginnings. However, the reluctance of reality to comply with the prospects of the regime made the restructuring of the festive calendar more and more sophisticated. They organized other manifestations involving public attendance near the undesirable festival, or even attempted unsubstantiated shifts of meaning of the celebrated event. For instance, on the occasion of the thoroughly planned 1848 commemorative festival, organized for the first time by the communists, a series of rival events were staged celebrating "one hundred years since the issue of the Communist Manifesto."[48]

The topic of "brotherhood" did not resume at all to the commemoration of the 1848 Revolution. It is a constant in the festive speeches given in different contexts, from the inauguration of the Progressive Youth organization to the visit of state officials in the county (during this period several members of the government were here, most frequently Vasile Luca[49] and Lucrețiu Pătrășcanu). On each occasion the officials addressed the issue of cooperation in highly ritualized and festive language, progressively dominating the public place. The festive character is argued by both the number and the variety of the public rituals. In the annual reports of various communist satellite organizations (Progressive Youth, Union Council of Covasna, Patriotic Defense, Workers Unique Front, SDP, and RCP) for 1946 are marked the following festivals:[50]

---

[46] Népi Egység [*People's Unity*], Sfântu Gheroghe, 15 March 1947.
[47] *Szabadság* [*Liberty*], Sfântu Gheroghe, 11 June 1945.
[48] ANJC, Fond 562, dosar nr.4/1948, f.18.
[49] Vasile Luca/László Luka was born in Covasna County.
[50] ANJC, Fond 561, dosar nr. 3/1947, f.1.

Date	Theme
21 January	Commemoration of Lenin's death
15–16 February	Commemoration of the Grivita strike
23 February	Red Army Day
6 March	One-year anniversary of the Groza government
8 March	Women's Day
15 March	Commemoration of the 1848 Revolution
1 May	Fighting for Democracy Day
10 May	National holiday, the manifestation of workers' unity
23 August	Soviet-Romanian armistice[67]
1 September	Two-year anniversary of activity of the United Unions
8 September	Commemoration of the *manisti* (right-wing group) attack against communists
20 October	ARLUS festival
7 November	Commemoration of the Great October Revolution
13 December	The struggle of the typography workers, Ana Pauker's birthday[68]
21 December	Stalin's birthday

The table includes only the festivals with a public character, involving a mass rally and qualifying as official public ritual. The spectrum of festive manifestations was much wider, including the "tenth anniversary of the release of the Communist Party (Bolshevik) of the Soviet Union's short history course," set up by intense propaganda and reported as a real success: "we have mobilized for this celebration a great number of participants."[53] Alongside these highly political public rituals were held religious processions, dance evenings, and club meetings, as well as numerous sport events, with communist activists valuing and exploiting the mobilizing resources of these manifestations.

Festivals, as means of cultural management, influence the behavioral dimension of ideology, as a way to change deep-seated moral orientations, "fixed by habit, custom and, often, by an older form of the ritual."[54] Therefore, the planning and through organization of the rituals has been largely described

---

[51] The armistice was signed on 12 September 1944.
[52] It was celebrated on 13 December even though Ana Pauker was born on 13 February.
[53] ANJC, Fond 561, dosar nr. 4/1948, f.79.
[54] Lane, C. *The Rites of Rulers: Ritual in Industrial Society – The Soviet Case*. Cambridge: Cambridge University Press, 1981, 2.

in the minutes of Party meetings. The importance of ritual can be quantified for the following indicators: the number of days the organizing committee has on disposal (the importance of the event being proportional to the number of days), the status and position in the Party of the involved members, the elaborateness of the plan, and so on. However, as the minutes and newspaper articles make clear, the most important indicator of success was the number of participants.

The attraction exercised on the population of the possibility to accede to the sacred realm, a possibility granted by public rituals, has been maintained by the new hegemonic force. The traditional structure of the festivals in this period was synchronized with the newly instituted message and symbolic order. Thus, as has been the tradition, the ritual cycle of a festival is inaugurated by fanfare in the early morning, followed by a religious service in one or more churches, a parade on the locality's main street towards the central stage, speeches, and laying wreaths on a monument. This official part usually is followed by the popular, joyful carnival, dance, and sport events. The national holidays are not yet secularized; thus the focus of ritual was on the religious service. The concept of festival is so deeply rooted in the moment of divine invocation in the collective mentalities that even the most secular festivals (e.g.,1 May) are centered on religious rites performed by a priest.[55]

23 August 1955. The military parade and the "joyful" demonstrators

"Democratic forces" restructured the festival's scenario according to the Soviet model. Thus the religious processions metamorphosed into "workers' demonstrations" but without altering the integrating functions of individuals to larger social units, setting up the framework in which individuals could

---

[55]   See the scenario of 1 May festival from Chichis. ANJC, Fond 562, dosar nr. 1/1946, f.4.

connect themselves to new identity structures. The inherent standardization and conformism of the ritual act and the largely related intentionality of the organizers makes the holistic presentation of the festivals futile and lacking analytic gains. Therefore, in what follows we will focus our attention on the festivals' "small deficiencies." Katherine Verdery, in her seminal book on Romanian national-communism, considers the regime's legitimacy to be resulting from "the nonorganization of an effective counterimage."[56] This presupposes not the consent of the whole population but the assent of part of the population and the lack of an alternative image backed by social forces in the discursive competition characteristic of the late 1940s. This period offers the advantages of accessible documentation; in the minutes of the meetings, the inconsistencies and organizational shortages were also (still) pointed out.

The organizers' concern was not only to professionally plan the technical aspects of the festivals but also to counteract potential manifestations deviating from the elaborated scenario.[57] Since every official public ritual is a test of legitimacy – considered an epiphany of abstract entities, the *face* of the Power – the risk for the symbolic economy of the organizers was substantial. Consequently, the commemoration of the 1848 Hungarian Revolution, for the first time organized by the Romanian Workers' Party in 1948, was a true test of organizational capacity: two delegates of Central Committee and the secretary of the county organization were present at the planning work shop. The meticulous delegation of responsibilities for each moment of the public ritual includes persons in charge of the mobilization of units from territory, activists in charge of placards, slogans, writing the guests' names; in charge of watching the stairs leading to the main stage, of the children who will give flowers.[58] The organizational efforts paid off: the commemoration was held without major incident, and participation was "significant." Precisely how significant it was cannot be determined, because while the Propaganda Department reported 7,000 participants, the Organizational Department counted only 4,500.

Organizational efforts are not the sole guarantee of success of the public rituals in a society where social control is not consolidated, due to its unknown variable: the voluntarism of public attendance. A lesson in humbleness was given by the proletariat itself, the "catalytic agent" of changes. In 1946, the Local Committee of the Unions planned a mass rally

---

[56] Verdery, K. *National Ideology under Socialism: Identity and Cultural Politics in Ceausescu's Romania.* Berkeley, Los Angeles, and London: University of California Press, 1995, 10.
[57] ANJC, Fond 562, dosar nr.4/1946, f.1.
[58] ANJC, Fond 562, dosar nr.1/1948, f.58.

on 1 September to mark two years of its existence. The declared aim was the "primary demonstrative character" of the public ritual, in order to "symbolize the workers' willpower."[59] However, at 10 o'clock there were twelve workers from the cigarette factory and forty from the textile factory, at a time when the number of union members in Sfântu Gheorghe exceeded 2,000. The president of the union, Viktor Nagy, refused to march through the city with a handful of workers, and in the end, the "festive" meeting was held in the union's building. In the union's search for an explanation for the failure, the RCP is criticized for the promised but not delivered organizational support. Therefore, there are two conclusions to be drawn from this failed festival. On the one hand, this sheds light on the real power the RCP had in the county. On the other hand, there are signs of tensions between the RCP and the union, and between the union and its members. The union-worker conflict had many phases: the leaders of the union were constantly changed, and leaders complained because of maltreatment, mocking and cursing, and they refused to accept a new candidacy.

Hobsbawm asserts that if the invented traditions lacked popular resonance, they failed to mobilize citizens volunteer.[60] In keeping with the imperative "new times – new heroes," and giving a human face to the new set of ideological values, steps were taken towards the construction of a myth biography. The life and death of Mihály Lázár met the requirements for the new hero: a mythological person with integrative effects on the newly constructed identity. Worker, communist, arrested for Party activity by the Hungarian authorities and beaten to death on 23 June 1941 – these were the foundational elements of the later proceedings. On 12 February 1945, during the symbolic restructuring of public space in the city, a downtown street was named after the hero. On 16 July 1945, the local newspaper *Szabadság* (*Liberty*) covered the commemoration of Mihály Lázár's martyrdom, the local Communist Party started fundraising in order to erect a statue, and a poem was written on the topic. However, after this promising start, the cult of the new hero after this promising start gradually declined and vanished.

The local Party elite belonged to a small social network. The frequent changes of leadership in the local communist organization and in the affiliated organizations reflected the rotation of cadres belonging to the same ethnic community and sharing a sense of local solidarity. Accordingly, the

---

59   ANJC, Fond 561, dosar nr.2/1946, f.19.
60   Hobsbawm, E. Mass-Producing Traditions: Europe, 1870–1914. In Hobsbawm, E., and Rangers, T. (eds.). *The Invention of Tradition.* Cambridge: Cambridge University Press, 1983, 263.

local SDP leaders blamed the new secretary of the local RCP, who originated from a different county, for the misunderstandings and tensions between the two political parties.[61] This structure of the leadership and the role of political leading force of the RCP in this structure projected the new nascent political culture: that of elitism in the administration of society.

The language in which the speeches are given is a continuous preoccupation of the organizers. In some cases the orators reflect on this aspect of the festive act, such as during the celebration of administrative reunification of the territory of Hăghig village, after the 29 May 1945 nullification of the Second Vienna Award. The president of the union, Viktor Nagy, later on the prefect of the county, points out to the participants that even though he is Hungarian, he will deliver his festive discourse in Romanian as a sign of his commitment to the idea of brotherhood and cooperation between the two nations.[62] The language of minorities is a serious impediment to the process of organizing the local Party units (cells), as well as imposing uniformity and control over their activity. When local organizations have to delegate representatives to higher forums, the candidate's ability to speak Romanian is always an issue. If someone refuses the candidacy due to a lack of language skills, a second delegate is nominated to interpret for him.[63] Therefore, there were organized courses for Party activists, and after their return, the minutes of the meetings reflect not only their language improvement but also uniformity in ideas and expressions, reconfiguring language into the "wooden language" of the regime.[64]

The duplicity of the ideological discourse is considered to be manifold and its taxonomic approach multi-layered. A distinction is made between the ideology expressed by the cognitive language involving the description of how reality is and the criteria of truth and falsity discussed above, and by the normative or prescriptive language of moral criteria.[65] Louis Althusser elaborated these characteristics and argued there was an interwoven set-up of the ideological speech-act by cognitive or "referential," "emotive," and "conative" categories.[66] This means a shift from a cognitive to an affective theory of ideology, which is not exclusive but rather inclusive. However, the presence of the affective elements in the ideological discourse appropriates the

---

[61] ANJC, Fond 552, dosar nr.5/1946, f.10.
[62] *Szabadság [Liberty]*, Sfântu Gheroghe, 3 June 1945, p.2.
[63] ANJC, Fond 561, dosar nr.2/1946, f.11.
[64] Thom, F. *Limba de lemn [Wooden language]*. Bucharest: Ed. Humanitas, 2005, 85.
[65] Eagleton, op. cit., 17.
[66] Althusser, L. *For Marx*. London: Verso, 1997, 214.

analysis of the ideological "text" embedded in the ritual of commemoration on the one hand. On the other hand, it supports the view of the communist ideological phenomena as using all the means of political legitimization: "they hammered at the whole keyboard."[67]

The language of discourses imposes a vision of the divided and irreconcilable world. This Manichaean view is, on the one hand, an inexhaustible source of metaphors and stereotypes. On the other hand, in the given historical context, it addresses a complex field of interpretation and horizon of expectations. One of the most frequently used slogans in various channels of communication is "Hungarian brother! The People's Unity is fighting for you!"[68] The linguistic construction bears the marks of the "wooden language" identified by Francoise Thom, but arguably the semantic register is not exhausted by considering it nothing more than an ideological vehicle. The message has a double semantic realm. First, "brother" is the term used in the *frontist* period to construct the identity of the "democratic forces"; thus it appeals to a socio-political explanatory paradigm, transgressing the national-ethnic taxonomy. This creates a sense of solidarity and of belonging to an effectively imagined group of democratic forces. The "fight" is waged against the Others, identified most often with "reactionaries" but also with "chauvinists" and "fascists." Secondly, somehow paradoxically, the "brother" is also Hungarian, an *exclusive* category, as non-Hungarians (i.e., Romanians) are excluded from this social group. But it is also *inclusive,* by projecting a sense of social solidarity over the entire ethnic community. This image of an inherently democratic ethnic community is a recurring topic of the discourses given by the leaders of the Hungarian People's Union, in their effort to negotiate the best possible status for the Hungarian minority, as well as in the minutes of the RCP and other organizations. In a 24 January 1945 report sent to the Organizational Committee of the United Union Movement (Mişcarea Sindicală Unită) by the union organization from Târgu Secuiesc, the author describes the achievements of the democratic organization as being blocked by the entrance of the "chauvinist Romanian authorities" in the city. The democratic transformation was completed after the expulsion of the Romanian authorities by the Soviet Command, in just two weeks, because "Hungarians are democratic in nature."[69] In a few months, the proletariat of

---

[67] Traschys, D. Symbols, Rituals, and Political Legitimation: Some Concluding Remarks. *Symbols of Power*, 175.

[68] *Népi Egység [People's Unity]*, Sfântu Gheroghe, 27 January 1947.

[69] ANJC, Fond 561, dosar nr. 1/1945, f.1.

this small town achieved communism, according to the image from the cited minute – an example of assimilating the reality to the ideological projection.

"Brotherhood" and "cooperation" are two adjacent conceptions, parts of a polysemic construction with a fuzzy and general referent. Accordingly, the role of justice is nothing else but the "consolidation of cooperation between different nations."[70] Imposing the political jargon, as with the use of "brother," took time. In the first year of "democracy," even the term "Mister" often appears in the minutes of the RCP.[71] The linguistic inventions are not automatically embraced; the linguistic *update* is made in the meetings and recorded in the minutes. Thus we know that by the transformation of the Progressive Youth into Communist Youth in Ozun village, they will address each other not as "brothers" but as "comrades" starting 28 August 1945.[72] In the same manner, Comrade Lajcsák points out to the participants at the meeting of the Workers Unity Front that, in line with Party directives, the term "peasant" will no longer be used there but will be replaced by "agricultural worker."[73] However, the ultimate illustration of the ritual function of language is the speech given by Colonel Saiev on the celebration of the national holiday in 1945. The speech was cheered by the participants, even though Colonel Saiev spoke in Russian...

The symbolic activities of the rituals are situated in a limited semantic range. In addition to the aforementioned acts of public ritual, the symbolic battle was waged over the use of national symbols. At first, the use of national symbols was not perceived as a threat by the organizers. In the minutes of the work-meeting to analyze the causes of the 23 August commemoration fiasco in 1945, there is a mention of the "rumor" spread by reactionaries that the use of national flags would be forbidden.[74] However, less than a year afterward, those who placed the national flag on the railway carriage on 1 May were labeled "provocateurs," and "chauvinists."[75] The waving of national flags at the grand meeting was blamed by the organizers (more than 500!) on "lack of vigilance."[76]

Aside from national symbols and the deeply rooted aspects of collective mentalities they stand for, there is a much wider variety of alternative

---

[70] Lucreţiu Pătrăşcanu, in a speech given during his visit to the county.
[71] *Szabadság [Liberty]*, Sfântu Gheorghe, 11 June 1945.
[72] ANJC, Fond 562, dosar nr.4/1946, f.93.
[73] ANJC, Fond 552, dosar nr.3/1945, f.4.
[74] ANJC, Fond 552, dosar nr.8/1947, f.20.
[75] ANJC, Fond 562, dosar nr.1/1945, f.74.
[76] ANJC Fond 562, dosar nr. 4/1946, f.4.

images of society competing with those projected by the official public rituals. The counter-images were constructed and disseminated in public space in a way generally labeled as "rumors." Festivals concentrate the manifestations of rumors around them by creating a symbolic discursive frame. People's attention is focused on realms of communication separated from everydayness; thus, public rituals arguably generate counter-images. In other words, the communicational patterns of festivals and rumors are identical. The very existence of these symbolic disapprovals is perceived by the organizers as a real threat to the participants' adhesion to the rites. The values and norms projected by the festivals and the identification with these projections, as well as the methodological nature of the ritual communication, pretend interpretative hegemony. The projection of the counter-images by rumors questions this hegemony. These images tend to have a powerful messianic and religious feature, to be a mythic projection rooted in the collective mentalities. One of the most powerful was the "Americans are coming to save us" myth, influencing often extreme social actions, such as the armed anticommunist resistance.[77] These mythical projections, though sometimes containing contradictory content, all had the same end: an alternative perception of reality. The offensive against rumors began in early 1945 with newspaper propaganda, interestingly enough, not by deconstructing them, but entering the logics imposed by these mythic projections and making reference to a traditional set of values, such as *good will* and *honesty*.

Rumors of "irredentism" were numerous and long-lasting due to their mobilizing effect on collective mentalities. In 1948, the Propaganda Department reported it had succeeded in quashing a rumor that Romania would be partitioned – that Hungary would annex Transylvania and the Soviet Union would annex the rest of Romania. The force of these images is demonstrated by their concrete effects: the peasants from Târgu Secuiesc and Baraolt delayed the harvest, and people from one village (Pava) started to stock gasoline, because it was scarcer in Hungary.[78] The fear of church closings generated mass psychosis. In more than one case, people came out of church crying, because they believed that by the next Sunday, the church would be destroyed. Unsurprisingly, the regime took severe measures against those who were identified as spreading rumors.

---

[77] Ibid., f.93.
[78] See Radosav, D. Rezistența anticomunistă armată din România între istorie și memorie. Ce-sereanu, R. (coord.). *Comunism și represiune în România. Istoria tematică a unui fratricid național.* Iași: Ed. Polirom, 2006, 82–99.

Consequently, the collective mentalities are structured by two dynamic vectors in discursive competition. On the one hand, there was a socially constructed image of reality and a horizon of expectation projected by the ritualized official festivals, with polymorph symbolic realm. On the other hand, there were the counter-images projected in the very same discursive system, but not as parts of the official discourse, and which had subversive forms of manifestation for the enforced symbolic order. The huge number of festivals celebrated in the period 1944–1948 indicates the symbolic struggle characteristic of times of crisis. The lack of an order established by a set of values grounded by social practice generates dynamic representations and overvalue concepts in a Manichaean and messianic interpretative system. Thinking about legitimacy, social control, and cultural management always presupposes a view that is inherently of those in charge. However, identity construction has never been the exclusive realm of social engineering. This paper argues that collective mentalities are not accessible from one analytic direction.

Ideological Pressure in School Lessons in the Estonian SSR

Eli Pilve

From the beginning of the Soviet occupation, education in Estonia was supervised by the People's Commissariat of Education. This institution was renamed the Ministry of Education of the Estonian Soviet Socialist Republic (ESSR) in 1946. It was supervised by the Central Committee of the Estonian Communist Party (hereinafter referred to as the ECP CC) and, in particular, by its Department of Education (in 1948–1951, however, education was relegated to the Department of Canvassing and Propaganda). The Department of Schools was responsible for ideological supervision and inspection of curricula and syllabi. Ideological upbringing was defined and understood as the process of developing a Soviet citizen who would be patriotic and ready to fight for communist ideas.[1] The *Sovietization* (i.e., changing the former system into a Soviet one) of Estonian education policies began in 1940–1941, when the Soviet system was enforced. It was rather formal and did not yet affect the actual content of education, but there was no escaping the changes in 1944–1953, when policies were adapted to those of the Russian SFSR.[2] In October 1944, during the re-occupation period in the autumn, most of the schools in continental Estonia were reopened. In 1944–1945 there were 198 primary schools, 790 seven-grade schools and thirty-eight secondary schools in Estonia.[3] In all, 4,405 teachers were hired to work at these schools. The number of primary schools increased, but that of the seven-grade schools decreased in subsequent years. By 1950, there were 7,500 teachers.[4]

---

[1] Raudsepp, A. Ajaloo õpetamise korraldus Eestis eesti õppekeeleg aüldhariduskoolis stalinismiajal (1944–1953). In Tannberg, T. (ed.). *Eesti NSV aastatel 1940–1953: Sovetiseerimise mehhanismid ja tagajärjed Nõukogude Liidu ja Ida-Euroopa arengute kontekstis.* Tartu: Eesti Ajalooarhiiv, 2007, 389–418.
[2] Raudsepp, op. cit., 10–11.
[3] Ibid., 22.
[4] Sirk, V. Haritlaskond osutus visaks vastaseks. *Tuna* 2004/1, 51–69, 61.

This article focuses on ideological education within the framework of various disciplines in Soviet schools, including the changed position of the teacher under these conditions. It does not comprise extracurricular activities, the work of the Pioneer organization and the Young Communist League. Ideological education in this paper concerns mainly the forced substitution of the former national values with new Soviet ones, the purpose of which was to make everybody feel that they were citizens of the empire and not, for example, Estonians or Latvians. The intention of this ideological education was to create a homogeneous population throughout the Soviet Union, with everybody having the same viewpoint, appreciation, and understanding.[5]

Minutes of ECP CC meetings, archival documents of the Ministry of Education of the ESSR – including reports by school inspectors stored in the National Archives of Estonia – and contemporary memoirs that can be found at the Estonian National Museum give us an idea of the means and measures adopted to create such a human being. Doctor Veronica Nagel[6] (Varik since 25 July 2009) has studied Soviet-era education in Estonia in greater detail. Historian Anu Raudsepp[7] has studied teaching history in a totally altered situation. Historian Tiiu Kreegipuu[8] has researched how history was used as a propaganda tool, along with researching the general management of culture in the Soviet era. David Branderberger,[9] a history professor at Richmond University who has studied Stalinist mass culture, should certainly also be mentioned, along with Jeffrey Brooks,[10] professor of European history at John Hopkins University, who has observed the development of Stalin's personality cult, and John Alexander Swettenham[11] from the War Museum of Canada.

---

[5] Kreegipuu, T. Ajaloo rakendamine propagandarelvana (History as a propaganda weapon). *Tuna* 3/2007, 46–69.

[6] Nagel, V. *Hariduspoliitika ja üldhariduskorraldus Eestis aastatel 1940–1991* (Education policies and management of general education in Estonia in 1940–1991). Tallinna Ülikooli sotsiaalteaduste dissertatsioonid, Tallinn, 2006.

[7] Raudsepp, A. *Ajaloo õpetamise korraldus Eesti NSV eesti õppekeelega üldhariduskoolides 1944–1985*. Tartu: Tartu Ülikooli Kirjastus, 2005, 10–11.

[8] Kreegipuu, T. *Nõukogude kultuuripoliitika printsiibid ja rakendused Eesti NSV-s aastatel 1944–1954 kirjanduse ja trükiajakirjanduse näitel. Magistritöö* (Principles and practices of Soviet cultural policies in the Estonian SSR in 1944–1954 based on examples from literature and the press. MA thesis). Tartu Ülikool, 2005; Kreegipuu, Ajaloo rakendamine, 46–69.

[9] Branderberger, D. *National Bolshevism: Stalinist Mass Culture and the Formation of Modern Russian National Identity 1931–1956.* Cambridge, MA, and London: Harvard University Press, 2002.

[10] Brooks, J. *Thank You, Comrade Stalin! Soviet Public Culture from Revolution to Cold War.* Princeton, NJ: Princeton University Press, 2001.

[11] Swettenham, J.A. *The Tragedy of the Baltic States: A Report Compiled from Official Documents and Eyewitnesses' Stories.* London: Hollis and Carter, 1954.

Compulsory education

Ten-year secondary school was established in the Soviet Union. For rural children, four grades were compulsory; for urban children it was seven. The general seven-year compulsory school was established in 1949.[12] Initially, in 1940–1941 primary school in Estonia remained a six-year school, as it had been in the Republic of Estonia. The former "pro-gymnasium" and "gymnasium" were combined to form the general secondary school. At first it retained its six-year period, meaning that the entire school period of primary and secondary education lasted for twelve years. The 1944 reform changed it into a four-year primary, seven-year or non-complete secondary school, and eleven-year secondary school. The additional year that differed from Russian schools was established on the pretext that intensive instruction in the Russian language was needed. (This was also done in Latvia, Lithuania, and Georgia.)[13] The eight-year basic school was established throughout the Soviet Union in 1959–1960, and the first basic-school graduate certificates were issued in 1962–1963.[14]

The re-adaptation of school instruction in the Estonian SSR: new curricula and textbooks

According to the second program of the Russian Communist (Bolshevik) Party passed in 1919 (which was in effect until the third program was passed in 1961), school was supposed to become an institution where a new generation was brought up that was capable of implementing communism once and for all.[15] The entire educational system was to be tied closely to communist propaganda. Curricula were to be drawn up to include a "special portion dedicated to the history of the Great October Revolution" and to explain the Soviet constitution.[16] Absolutely every subject had to indoctrinate the pupil ideologically and politically.[17] David Branderberger believes

---

[12] Karjahärm, T., and Sirk, V. *Kohanemine ja vastupanu. Eesti haritlaskond 1940–1987*. Tallinn: Argo, 2007, 76.

[13] Nagel, op. cit., 50.

[14] Karjahärm and Sirk, op. cit., 81.

[15] Venemaa Kommunistliku (bolševike) Partei programm. *NLKP kongresside, konverentside ja Keskkomitee pleenumite resolutsioonid ja otsused I*. Tallinn: Eesti Riiklik Kirjastus, 1956, 409–454.

[16] Ibid., 449–451; Must, A. Koguteos "Marx-Engels-Lenin-Stalin kultuurist ja kasvatusest." *Eesti Bolševik : EK(b)P KK ajakiri*, 1947/24, 63–66.

[17] Ideelis-poliitilise kasvatuse küsimused nõukogude koolis. *Eesti Bolševik*, 1946/17, 215–221.

the main points of Soviet ideological upbringing to be the following: first, the popularization of suitable pre-revolutionary historical events and heroes; second, Russian orientation, because in parallel with declaring Soviet patriotism and friendship between nations, Soviet ideology actually bore the message of the superiority of the Russian people; and third, Stalin's personality cult.[18] All that was also reflected in school instruction, first and foremost in textbooks.

A temporary curriculum was drawn up for the 1940–1941 academic year. The main emphasis in history was on the history of the formation of the Soviet Union. The physical map of the Soviet Union and economic geography were added to the geography curriculum. Reading material describing the life and working conditions of the working people was included in the literary program, and special emphasis was placed on revolution-era poetry.[19]

Examination at Koeru Secondary School, 1950. On the blackboard is a slogan: "We greet the great Russian nation!" Source: Estonian Film Archives (EFA) 204.0-3011.

---

[18]   Branderberger, op. cit., 93.
[19]   Nagel, op. cit., 20.

The number of lessons was increased for mathematics and chemistry. The fundamentals of Darwinism were added to the natural science curriculum for the three highest grades. The teaching of *kodulugu* (homeland studies) was discontinued in elementary grades, since its nationalist content contradicted Soviet ideology. Religious instruction, Latin, Greek, civics, and philosophy were left out of the curriculum, while Russian, the Stalinist constitution, and the aforementioned history and geography of the Soviet Union were added. Physical education had to be tied to military training.[20]

Since the existing textbooks did not correspond to the new ideological conditions and the publication of suitable textbooks took time, the first task was the revision of existing textbooks. Teaching materials that had been in use earlier received permission for further use only if certain contents were removed in textbook reprints. These included texts where increases in the price of food were calculated, where the proper name of the Republic of Estonia was used, or where events were mentioned that did not suit the Soviet treatment of history.[21] Revised textbooks were supplied with selected texts about Lenin, Stalin, the Great October Revolution, the Red Army, heroes of labor and Stakhanovites, kolkhozes (collective farms), pioneers, and other such topics.[22]

The regulation issued on 27 December 1944 by the Estonian SSR Council of People's Commissars (hereinafter referred to as the ESSR CPC) and the ECP CC already demanded the complete removal of all former textbooks.[23] The question of ideology was the top priority in publishing new textbooks, and the Party and government supervised the publication.[24] As was said: "The first unconditional requirement concerning textbooks is the complete assurance of the communist direction."[25]

More thoroughly prepared curricula were adopted in 1948. They were even more ideologized than the temporary curriculum of 1940, and pressure

---

20   Ibid.
21   R. Aavakivi's review of the textbooks: Etverk, E., and Rägo, G., Matemaatika õpik humanitaar-gümnaasiumile; Ratassepp, K., and Rägo, G., Matemaatika harjutustik gümnaasiumile, I klassi kursus; Ratassepp, K., and Rägo, G., Matemaatika harjutustik gümnaasiumile, II klassi kursus; Ratassepp, K., and Rägo, G., Matemaatika harjutustik gümnaasiumile, III klassi kursus, 30 August 1940, ERA. R-14.1.300, 23.
22   Swettenham, op. cit., 107–108.
23   Regulation issued by the Estonian SSR Council of People's Commissars and the Estonian Communist Party Central Committee concerning improving the work of schools, 27 December 1944. *Eesti NSV Ülemnõukogu ja Valitsuse Teataja 1945*, 2, 23.
24   Nagel, op. cit., 52.
25   Jessipov, B., and Gontšarov, N. *Pedagoogika*. Õpik pedagoogilistele koolidele II. Tartu: Pedagoogiline Kirjandus, 1947, 161.

continued to increase. While the use of textbooks compiled in the Republic of Estonia continued to be allowed until 1949–1950 in many subjects while new textbooks were being prepared, now even Soviet-era textbooks compiled in Estonia were to be eliminated. Nevertheless, quite a few textbooks compiled in Estonia remained in use as before. During the 1952–1953 academic year, forty-five of the 115 textbooks in use had been written in the Estonian SSR, while the remainder were translations of textbooks from the Russian SFSR, including history textbooks.[26]

"Correct" teaching

History

History classes were placed under more scrutiny and control than other subjects. "History is a Party subject,"[27] one publication declared. "One of the most important tasks while teaching history is instruction in Soviet patriotism."[28] Instead of the name "Russian history," the discipline was called "history of the USSR," and instruction was to become even more patriotic.[29]

The new history syllabus for 1948 increased the number of class periods for history by 122. History was taught for 748 periods during the eight years of basic school: 405 of these periods were meant for the history of the USSR and 343 for general history. A year later the number of history periods increased to 795. The elementary program began in the fourth grade, where the main focus was on the personality of Stalin. The fifth grade studied the ancient Orient and Greece, the seventh grade reached the Middle Ages, and the teaching of modern history began in the eighth grade and continued in the ninth, when the history of the union republics up to the year 1613 was also introduced. The tenth grade continued with the latter (until the end of the nineteenth century), and the eleventh grade studied the history of the USSR and contemporary history.[30] Everything before 1917 was described as the prologue to the Great October Revolution.[31]

Until 1948–1949, the final exam had to be taken in general history, but later it was in the history of the USSR. This was not much of a change, since

[26] Raudsepp, 2007, 391–392.
[27] Stražev, A.I. Ajaloo õpetamine koolis, meie noorsoo ideelis-poliitilise ja kõlbelise kasvatuse võima srelv. *Nõukogude Kool* 1947/8–9, 483–492.
[28] Ibid, 487.
[29] Raudsepp, 2007, 396–397.
[30] Ibid., 399–401.
[31] Swettenham, op. cit., 108.

even under the previous format, three of the four questions were about the USSR.[32]

David Branderberger has pointed out that in the second half of the 1940s, propaganda focused more and more pointedly on Russia and the Russian language. The culture and history of the Russian people dominated, and the culture and role of the other union republics were forgotten and not spoken about.[33] In Estonia, local history was not taught in schools either, according to the ECP Bureau decision of 12 September 1945. The same decision terminated the ESSR People's Commissariat of Education's commission from the Tartu University History Department to draw up a thirty-five-period program of Estonian history for eleventh-grade secondary school pupils. The same decision prescribed the establishment of a commission for compiling a new Marxist syllabus and textbook of Estonian history. The commission consisted of professors Hans Kruus, Richard Kleis, Harri Moora, senior lecturer Hilda Moosberg, and Villem Orav, the methodology expert at the ESSR People's Commissariat of Education. The syllabus was to be completed by 15 September of the same year, the theses of the textbook by 15 November, and the textbook manuscript by 15 January 1946. Kruus and Moosberg were sent to Moscow to consult specialists in Baltic history there.[34] However, the decision was repealed in the syllabus for 1946, which only allowed a few periods for local history in between the lessons on USSR history.[35]

It was not until 1948 that the adopted syllabus allowed teaching Estonian history in the fourth and eleventh grades only if the new textbook were to be completed by then. Since the textbook was not even being written yet, the issue of Estonian history was shelved indefinitely. The editor of the missing textbook, however, was confirmed: Gustav Naan.[36] When the Department of Estonian History was done away with in the summer of 1949, Estonian history was no longer taught in basic and secondary schools. (At the end of the 1940s and the beginning of the 1950s, local history was no longer taught in the other two Baltic republics either.)[37] Tartu University historians raised the issue of reviving the teaching of Estonian history immediately after Stalin's death, but it was first discussed publicly at a conference of history teachers

---

[32] Raudsepp, 2007, 401.
[33] Branderberger, op. cit., 196.
[34] Eesti ajaloo õpetamisest ENSV koolides (About teaching Estonian history in Estonian SSR schools), 12 September 1945, ERAF.1.4.206, 11–12.
[35] Raudsepp, 2007, 398.
[36] Keskkoolide ENSV ajaloo õpiku küsimusest (About the issue of secondary school ESSR history textbook), 21 September 1950, ERAF.1.4.1028, 168; Raudsepp, 2007, 401–402.
[37] Raudsepp, 2007, 402–403, 408–409.

organized by the Tartu University History Department in the spring of 1954. In 1955, Karl Laigna, a lecturer at the Tartu University History Department, compiled a program for teaching Estonian history at general education schools, but the ESSR Ministry of Education did not grant it approval. Some Tartu schools, though, attempted to teach according to this program. Estonian history was officially taught again in 1957–1958 (forty periods), and unofficially, attempts to do so had been made earlier at several schools.[38] The layout of the first Estonian history textbook was completed in 1957.[39]

Literature

In order to teach "correct" history, literature programs were also changed. Educator Aleksander Elango said that this was influenced by the All-Union C(b)P CC decisions of 14 August 1946 concerning the journals *Zvezda* and *Leningrad*.[40] Actually, there was nothing new in these decisions, which reproached the editorial offices of those journals for forgetting the Leninist principle: a journal could not be apolitical. Publications had to observe Soviet politics, since they were meant to be a powerful tool in the upbringing of the young. The Soviet system could not and would not tolerate indifference or ideological neutrality in this important task. Soviet literature was hailed as the most progressive in the world, as it bore in mind only the interests of the state and its people. This literature was to assist the state in bringing up an aware generation of young people who believed in what they did and were not afraid to face difficulties. "Art for art's sake," apolitical and non-ideological literature, was considered alien to the Soviet people and harmful to the state.[41]

Geography

Geography was also considered highly important for carrying out ideological instruction and upbringing. Aleksander Valsiner, deputy to the ESSR People's Commissar for Education, published the article "Socio-Political Upbringing at School" in the February 1941 issue of the journal *Nõukogude Kool* and explained the directives of the Commissariat for the third-, fourth-, and sixth-grade geography classes. The teacher was obligated to focus on economic

---

[38] Ibid., 90.

[39] *Eesti NSV ajalugu: õpik keskkooli IX–XI klassile.* Tallinn: Riiklik kirjastus, 1957.

[40] Elango, A. *Pedagoogika ajalugu.* Tallinn: Valgus, 1984, 227.

[41] Постановление Оргбюро ЦК ВКП(б) "О журналах "Звезда" и "Ленинград"" 14 августа 1946 г. *Московский Государственный Университет им. М. В. Ломоносова,* http://www.hist.msu.ru/ER/Etext/USSR/journal.htm, 14.01.2009.

geography for two-thirds of the periods, and the rest had to be dedicated to political and physical regional geography of the USSR. Only two periods were set aside for the geography of the ESSR, and during these two periods, a survey of the construction of building socialism was to be taught. The directives explicitly stated that in the lessons about the ESSR, the bourgeois system had to be criticized. It should be emphasized that the land reform of 1919 did not offer any solution "for the working peasants' interests," and since industry was developed incorrectly, unemployment resulted. On the other hand, it had to be shown that the "working people's revolution of 21 June 1940 set the economy on the right track and achievements were soon to follow."[42]

Geography lesson, Paide, 1947. Source: EFA 204.0-1153.

Foreign languages
For example, the 1952 English textbook for the eighth grade opens with a patriotic text about the birthplace of Stalin.[43] The message of the texts is quite clear: the Soviet Union has the largest number of good children's authors in

---

[42] Directives for forms 3, 4, and 6 geography syllabi, a circular, 17 February 1941, ERAR.1013.1.217, unpaged.

[43] Belova, J., and Todd, L. *Inglise keele õpik VIII klassile. English Textbook. Form Eight.* Tallinn: Estonian State Publishers, 1952, 3–4.

the world, whereas American children have to read comic books that poison their young minds. No comic-book superhero would be strong enough to defeat America's rampant crime. The American government, however, does nothing to protect children. Warmongers as they are, they long for a new war, and the children of today will be the army of tomorrow.[44] The German textbook of 1950 includes a text dedicated to the anniversary of the Red Army, including the slogans *Es lebe die Sowjetarmee!* (Long Live the Soviet Army!), *Es lebe die Sowjetflotte!* (Long live the Soviet Navy!), and *Es lebe die Sowjet luftflotte!* (Long live the Soviet Air Force!).[45]

Music and art

Music and art had to be used to instill patriotism and internationalism as well. "The teacher explains to the pupils the significance of Russian classical music and tells them what influence Russian composers and painters have had on foreign artists..."[46] The compulsory repertoire of music instruction included the "The Internationale," "The Marsellaise," "Red Banner," "Dead March" and "Song for the Motherland." There were additional optional songs like "Comintern," "Song of Stalin," "Song of Voroshilov," "March of the Workers' Army," "Song of the Common Front," and several others of the kind.[47] Leelo Tamm, a pupil in the basic compulsory school Nr. 8, remembers that when they all had to sing "The Internationale" at the morning assembly, she never joined in, but she could not help liking the dynamic melodies by Isaac Dunayevsky and some other contemporary Soviet composers.[48]

Chemistry, physics, and mathematics

Science teachers had to speak first of all about *our country's* technology, the importance of chemistry in national defense, and the life and work of Soviet scientists,[49] who, unlike the scientists of capitalist countries, were happy to have enough work and were respected for it. Teachers of physics and chemistry had to try much harder than those who taught mathematics. They did get a few short biographies of carefully selected Russian scientists and the

---

[44] Ibid. 8–11.

[45] Petrenko, M., and Jastržembskaja, M. *Saksa keele õpik VI klassile*. Tallinn: Eesti Riiklik Kirjastus, 1951, 62.

[46] Gruzdev, op. cit., 99.

[47] Üldlauluvara keskkoolidele 1940/41 kooliaastaks (Songs for secondary schools in 1940–1941), 16 September 1940, ERAR.14.1.48, 26.

[48] Eesti Rahva Muuseum (Estonian National Museum, further on ERM) KV 783, 416–417.

[49] Gruzdev, op. cit., 99.

story of the electrification of the vast homeland.[50] As early as 1951, an article was published in the paper *Nõukogude Õpetaja* reminding physics teachers not to forget their duty to bring their pupils up in the spirit of the materialist world outlook.[51] It was a bit easier for mathematics teachers, as the textbook exercises already contained comparisons of the most backward workers' daily quotas with those of the Stakhanovites.[52] "The language of numbers is convincing, and it is necessary for the mathematics teacher to use statistical data of socialist construction like teachers of history and geography do," stressed an article in *Nõukogude Õpetaja* on 21 September 1951.[53]

From personality cult to Party cult

In February 1956, Nikita Khrushchev gave his speech at the closed night session of the CPSU 20th Congress concerning Stalin's personality cult and its consequences. Even though he did not condemn mass terror as a whole, this speech nevertheless had an effect, easing the atmosphere of fear and making society slightly more liberal.[54]

After the personality cult was condemned, it was simply replaced by the Party cult.[55] A graphic example of this is the concluding sentences of the different editions of the *History of the Estonian SSR from Earliest Times to the Present*. The first edition, published in 1952, ends with the statement of conviction: "There is no greater joy, say the Estonian people, than to build communism in the harmonious family of the peoples of the Soviet Union under the ingenious leadership of Comrade Stalin."[56] In the project of the second edition (1956), Stalin is replaced by the Party: "There is no greater joy, say the Estonian people, than to build communism in the harmonious

---

[50] See, e.g., Sokolov, I. *Füüsika X klassile: Elekter.* Tallinn, Eesti Riiklik Kirjastus, 1952; Levtšenko, V., Ivantsova, M., Solovjov, N., and Feldt, V. *Keemia X klassile.* Tallinn, Eesti Riiklik Kirjastus, 1952.

[51] Jelizarov, K. Õpilaste maailmavaate kujunemine. *Nõukogude Õpetaja*, 1951/36, 7 September 1951, 3.

[52] Rünk, O., and Roos, H. *Matemaatika õpik V klassile. II vihik.* Tallinn, Pedagoogiline Kirjandus, 1948, 25.

[53] Kommunistlikust kasvatusest matemaatikatunnis (S. Ponomarjovi järgi). *Nõukogude Õpetaja*, 1951/38, 21 September 1951, 4.

[54] Kuuli, O. *Sula ja hallad Eesti NSV-s: Kultuuripoliitikast aastail 1953–1969.* Tallinn: O. Kuuli, 2002, 60.

[55] Raudsepp, 2005, 67–68, 74.

[56] Naan, G. (ed.). *Eesti NSV ajalugu (kõige vanemast ajast tänapäevani).* Tallinn: Eesti Riiklik Kirjastus, 1952, 464.

family of the peoples of the Soviet Union under the wise leadership of the Communist Party."[57]

The change in cult object did not lead to any significant change in content. The dogma of the communist view of the world as the one and only true teaching remained in effect; the principle of culture, literature, and art as means for ideological and political educational work, the requirement of socialist realism, and other such characteristics.[58] Education was turned into a training school where ideological truth was self-evidently known; it was not necessary or even allowed to seek such truth.[59] In that sense, ideological indoctrination in Soviet schools remained unchanged until the end. When the ideological and political indoctrination of pupils again appeared on the agenda at the meeting of the teachers' council of Tallinn Secondary School No. 1 on 25 March 1974, one decision made it obligatory to "teach pupils to relate critically to their opinions that are not in harmony with established truths."[60]

Yet in the somewhat more liberal conditions after Stalin's death and Khrushchev's speech denouncing Stalinism, opinions could nevertheless be expressed to a certain extent concerning the content of textbooks. Teachers expressed dissatisfaction with their dry text, overabundance of detail, and the fact that they did not take local conditions into account. For instance, biology and zoology textbooks meant for use throughout the Soviet Union did not contain material concerning cultivated plants that grew in Estonia and species of animals that lived there. The situation concerning foreign-language textbooks was particularly problematic. They were also translated from Russian and thus in their original form were meant for Russian-speaking pupils.[61] The educational system reform of 1958–1959 did allow more original textbooks to be written in the union republics. This opportunity was used zealously in Estonia, so that by the mid-1960s, 97 original textbooks and 33 translated textbooks were in use in local general education schools. The CPSU CC and the USSR Council of Ministers obligated the USSR Ministry of Education to work together with the local ministries in publishing new textbooks in connection with the subsequent transition to new curricula. In

---

[57] Naan, G. (ed.). *Eesti NSV ajalugu: kõige vanemast ajast tänapäevani: projekt arutamiseks.* Tallinn: Eesti Riiklik Kirjastus,1952, 464

[58] Karjahärm and Sirk, op. cit., 231–232; Raudsepp, 2005, 68.

[59] Karjahärm and Sirk, op. cit., 76.

[60] Tallinn Secondary School No. 1 Educational Council book of minutes, 8 May 1973–29 September 1974, TLA. R-205.1.95, 62–63.

[61] Nagel, op. cit., 71.

reality, however, the constrainment of local interests began again. Figures in the field of education in Estonia led by Minister of Education Ferdinand Eisen nevertheless succeeded in preserving original textbooks, which was quite rare in the Soviet Union.[62]

Ideological pressure. Weakening and re-strengthening

The decrease in the membership of the Komsomol and Pioneer organizations in schools was a main feature of the liberalization that took place in society after Stalin's death and Khrushchev's speech. The number of Komsomol members in Estonia was 11,464 during the 1952–1953 academic year. By 1956–1957 it had already dropped to 9,256. The number of Pioneers dropped correspondingly from 63,049 to 50,750. Teachers became bolder and the proportion of ideological indoctrination dropped, in both subject lessons and the weekly sessions with the homeroom teacher.[63] Teachers' councils dealt less and less with ideological questions, focusing mainly on teaching. If we compare the minutes of teachers' council meetings at Tallinn Secondary Schools Nos. 1, 7, and 22, the periods before and after Stalin's death are clearly differentiated. Before 1953, the question of showing the indoctrinational aspect in lesson outlines, the observance of Soviet holidays, questions concerning the ideological professional development of teachers, and other such matters are consistently included on the agendas in the minutes of teacher's council meetings. Both teachers and principals often made presentations of an ideological nature (for instance, on topics like "The Teaching of History in Soviet Schools," "The Cultivation of the Communist View of the World through Subject Lessons," and so on). At least at Secondary School No. 7, the Party organization decided on these presentations. Most of the time, teachers of the Russian language or history teachers were asked to give lectures, because they were often also Party members.[64]

By April 1953, the situation in teachers' council minutes is entirely different. There are no longer any ideological lectures at all, only the major Soviet holidays remain, and even the reflection of preparations for them is more vague and indefinite; the ideological indoctrination of pupils is rarely mentioned, and then only in a cursory fashion. The political self-education

---

[62] Raudsepp, 2005, 41–46.
[63] Ibid., 32–34.
[64] Interview with Kristi Tarand, 18 August 2011.

of teachers, however, remains on the agenda. Ideological presentations return to the minutes of teachers' council meetings in 1970–1972 but significantly less frequently than during Stalin's lifetime. Even though the difference before and after 1953 is noticeable in the minutes from all three schools mentioned, everything nevertheless depended on the school, on its leadership and teachers. For instance, at least judging by the minutes, Tallinn Secondary School No. 1 was the most loyal. The Stalin-era minutes at Tallinn Secondary Schools Nos. 7 and 22 are comparable to the post-Stalin- era minutes at Secondary School No. 1 in terms of the frequency of introduction of ideology.[65] English teacher Kristi Tarand from Secondary School No. 7 recalls that generally speaking, most ideological indoctrination was reduced to paperwork. The ideological aim of the lesson had to be entered into the lesson plan, and those plans were checked as well, but in practice, those lesson plans were not followed in the classroom.[66]

The CPSU CC Presidium passed the decision "Concerning the Personality Cult and Over coming Its Consequences" on 30 June 1956. This decision criticized Stalin's personality cult yet emphasized that this did not change the socialist nature of Soviet society. The aim of the decision was to blunt the effect of Khrushchev's speech to the Twentieth CPSU Congress. The release of political prisoners nevertheless continued in 1956–1957, and some of them were rehabilitated as well. At the same time, pro-independence sentiments strengthened in several places. Unrest broke out in Poland in the summer of 1956, and dozens of people were killed in the suppression of this unrest. Demonstrations broke out among the people in Hungary in October and November of 1956, developing into a real uprising, the suppression of which required extensive intervention by Soviet armed forces. On the background of these events, the pressure that had slightly abated began gathering strength again.[67] The education provided in Estonia was criticized at the Tenth ECP Congress in 1958. More effective ideological indoctrination of young people was demanded, emphasizing the importance of lessons in social sciences,

---

[65] Tallinn Secondary School No. 1 educational council minutes, 21 November 1944–25 June 1985, TLA.R-205.1, files 1, 3, 4, 7, 9, 12, 16, 23, 33, 41, 64, 78, 95, 102, 112, 116, 122, 126, 127, 133, 138, 141, 144, 148; Tallinn Secondary School No. 7 educational council minutes, 24 April 1945–22 June 1985, TLA.R-191.1, files 5, 26, 42, 50, 71, 62, 88, 103, 114, 131, 138, 195, 227; Tallinn Secondary School No. 22 educational council minutes, 16 October 1944–2 November 1982, TLA.R-220.1, files 1, 7, 10, 13, 15, 17, 21, 22, 28, 40, 52, 64, 115, 136a, 146a, 156, 108, 177a, 185, 192.

[66] Interview with Kristi Tarand, 18 August 2011.

[67] Kuuli, op. cit., 62–63.

literature, art, and history in this work.[68] Even after nearly twenty years of occupation, the reign of terror had not made families politically reliable, and the push to establish boarding schools as an effective method of ideological indoctrination of Soviet children and young people began. There were three such schools in Estonia as of 1958.[69] In the Program of the CPSU was said, that "Communist education is based on the public upbringing of children."[70] Since the home did not provide children with sufficient examples in some issues related to upbringing, boarding schools were expected to do this work.[71]

Party organizations in schools were considered weak, and in many places they did not even exist. The Estonian Leninist Communist Youth Society Central Committee (hereinafter referred to as ELKNÜ CC) First Secretary Vaino Väljas accused the Ministry of Education of incompetence in selecting teaching staff and in strengthening the Komsomol and Pioneer organizations. ECP CC Secretary Leonid Lentsman admitted that in addition to the indoctrination of young people, indoctrination work among teachers had also been neglected.[72] Thereafter, agitation for teachers to join the Party began to receive greater attention. "Party organizations in schools have to fight to prevent apolitical people from teaching young people," said Vaino Väljas.[73] While teachers who were Party members formed 17 percent of the entire body of teachers as late as 1961, that proportion had already risen to 36 percent by 1966.[74] This proportion was 55 percent among history teachers in 1965.[75]

The CPSU CC passed a decision in 1979 "Concerning the Further Improvement of Work in Ideology and Political Indoctrination," which obligated the union republics to assure a high scientific level of propaganda and agitation; to make the practicality and concreteness of propaganda and

---

[68] Eestimaa Kommunistliku Partei X kongress. *Noorte Hääl*, no. 24–25, 29–30 January 1958; Võitluses NLKP XX kongressi ajalooliste otsuste täitmise eest: Eestimaa Kommunistliku Partei X kongress. *Noorte Hääl*, no. 26, 31 January 1958.

[69] Raudsepp, 2005, 30, 36–37.

[70] Nõukogude Liidu Kommunistliku Partei programm (vastu võetud NLKP XXII kongressi poolt). Tallinn: Eesti Riiklik Kirjastus, 1961, 114.

[71] Sõer, J. Õppe- ja kasvatustöö kooliinternaadis, ERA.R-2216.2.48, 28–29.

[72] Eestimaa Kommunistliku Partei X kongress. *Noorte Hääl*, no. 24–25, 29–30 January 1958; Võitluses NLKP XX kongressi ajalooliste otsuste täitmise eest: *Noorte Hääl*, no. 26, 31 January 1958.

[73] Väljas, V. Õppe-kasvatustööst ja selle parandamisest Tallinna üldhariduslikes koolides NLKP XXII kongressi otsuste valgusel. Sarri, G. (ed.). *Koolide parteiorganisatsioonide töökogemusi. Artiklite kogumik*. Tallinn: Eesti Riiklik Kirjastus, 1963, 32–53, 46.

[74] Raudsepp, 2005, 30.

[75] Ibid., 39.

agitation more effective by applying its connection to life and to economic and political tasks; to develop the attacking nature of propaganda and agitation.[76] This was yet another pages-long decision whose content offered nothing new. According to historians Toomas Karjahärm and Väino Sirk, it seemed that during the Brezhnev era, the regime itself did not even try to get the people to believe official ideology. All that was required was for people to express themselves "correctly." Karjahärm and Sirk consider the increase in the educational level of employees to be one possible reason for this.[77] Kalju Luts, the deputy minister of education at that time, similarly recalls that the entire Soviet state was built on the principle of appearances:

> There were certain rules of the game that had to be played at every level, and reality, which depended on the people who governed that reality. Thus the Ministry of Education had two deputy ministers; one who dealt with issues concerning content, and the other who made sure that the ideological aspect would also be displayed. This was a practical system where appearances and reality existed in a harmony in which they did not disturb one another.[78]

This kind of situation, however, did leave its mark in people's psyches. Soviet citizens developed two parallel self-images. One was familiar and was thought of in reality but, as a rule, was not allowed to be shown outwardly; the other corresponded to requirements. Historian Richard Pipes maintains that people adapted to the parallel existence of appearance and reality by splitting their personalities, thus finding themselves in a schizophrenic situation. On the one hand, people knew what was true, but that was suppressed – shared only with one's closest family members and friends. On the other hand, people pretended to believe every word of official propaganda. This also left a psychological heritage that lasted longer than communism itself. Lying became a means of survival, and it is only a small step to go from lying to cheating.[79]

Both the liberation movement and pressure for its suppression were activated in the 1980s. History and social studies teacher Vilma Kahk from Tallinn Secondary School No. 21 recalls that men from the security organs came to the school more and more often to give lectures in those days. The school principal of that time resigned as a result of the constant checking and

---

76 NLKP Keskkomitees. NLKP Keskkomitee otsus "Ideoloogia- ja poliitilise kasvatustöö edasi-
    sest parandamisest." *Rahva Hääl*, no. 105, 6 May 1979.
77 Karjahärm and Sirk, op. cit., 297.
78 Interview with Kalju Luts, 28 June 2011.
79 Pipes, R. *Kommunism: Lühiajalugu*. Tartu: Ilmamaa, 2005, 85 (original: Pipes, R. *Commu-
    nism. A History*. New York: Random House, 2001).

control to which the school was subjected. The principal wished to be relieved of the unbearable pressure and also to create the impression that at least one head had rolled, thus sparing the school from more serious problems.[80]

Russification

Even though serious Russification policy began in the 1970s, greater attention was paid to the teaching of Russian even earlier. Officially, the study of Russian in Estonian schools was voluntary. In reality, the teaching of Russian was scrutinized more than any other subject. This is also clearly expressed in the teachers' council minutes at schools, where Russian is regularly focused on from the beginning while other subjects get individual attention only rarely.[81] The pressure to learn Russian was so great that in practice it was not possible for pupils to decide not to study it. This did, however, make it possible for pupils to take a careless attitude towards the subject, because a student could fail an elective subject and still not be held back. Kristi Tarand worked as a teacher for twenty-five years, and she recalls only one case in her entire teaching career where a pupil refused to take Russian because he found out that it was an elective subject, so to speak. The school leadership wanted to expel him from school because of that, but no airtight excuse could be found, and so he was simply forced to transfer to another school. This happened in about 1960, recalls Tarand.[82]

When the Estonian SSR teachers' congress passed a decision in 1967 to make the study of Russian mandatory, the USSR Ministry of Education rejected the decision under the reasoning that the Russian language had such great authority that no coercion was needed to convince people to learn it.[83]

---

[80] Interview with Vilma Kahk, 17 May 2010; Kross, E.N. Kuidas Raua tänava koolis algas N Liidu lagunemine. Kross, E.N. *Vabaduse väravad: valiktekste 1988–2006*. Tartu: Ilmamaa, 2007, 17.

[81] Tallinn Secondary School No. 1 educational council minutes, 21 October 1944–25 June 1985, TLA.R-205.1, files 1, 3, 4, 7, 9, 12, 16, 23, 33, 41, 64, 78, 95, 102, 112, 116, 122, 126, 127, 133, 138, 141, 144, 148; Tallinn Secondary School No. 7 educational council minutes, 24 April 1945–22 June 1985, TLA.R-191.1, files 5, 26, 42, 50, 71, 62, 88, 103, 114, 131, 138, 195, 227; Tallinn Secondary School No. 22 educational council minutes, 16 October 1944–2 November 1982, TLA.R-220.1, files 1, 7, 10, 13, 15, 17, 21, 22, 28, 40, 52, 64, 115, 136a, 146a, 156, 108, 177a, 185, 192.

[82] Interview with Kristi Tarand, 18 August 2011.

[83] Nagel, op. cit., 87.

While work had focused on intensifying the teaching of Russian until the 1970s, now bilingualism became the slogan. The promotion of learning other foreign languages disappeared in parallel with this. Non-Russians had to know Russian just as well as their own mother tongue. The creation of mixed kindergartens was seen as one possibility for fostering this. The authorities also wanted to establish mixed schools, but this idea was abandoned (except for areas where such schools had naturally come into being due to Estonians and Russians living together in the same area, such as Kehra, Sindi, and Maardu). The requirement of bilingualism was taken so seriously that in the early 1970s, even in mathematics lessons, the Russian equivalent for every new term had to be given to pupils whenever a new mathematical term was introduced. The actual implementation of this requirement, however, depended on the teacher.[84] Kristi Tarand also remembers this kind of pressure. In order to comply with this requirement, she would essentially have had to teach two foreign languages simultaneously. She simply did not do so and continued to teach only English.[85] As it was, the number of hours of instruction in Russian was increased in the curriculum of 1978 at the expense of other foreign languages, including English.[86] Indeed, the Soviet Union's minister of education, M. Prokofjev, could not understand why it was necessary for Estonians to continue to study their mother tongue at all at the secondary-school level in Estonian-language schools. He also felt that too many of hours of instruction were dedicated to Estonian literature. After the head of the USSR Ministry of Education Main Administration for Schools J. Ivanov met with ECP CC Secretary V. Väljas, who was in favor of teaching the Estonian language and literature at the secondary school level, Prokofjev also finally agreed to the continued teaching of Estonian.[87]

Karl Vaino, an Estonian from Russia, was appointed to head the ECP in 1978. He willingly went along with Russification policy. He did not even use the word "Estonian," preferring the word *eestimaalane* ("resident of Estonia").[88] Rein Ristlaan became the ECP CC ideology secretary in 1980, and he was very much in favor of mixed kindergartens and schools as well. Thus as of 1981, the teaching of Russian began in the first grade in Estonian schools and in some Estonian kindergartens as well.[89]

---

[84] Interview with Sirje and Taavet Kuurber, 22 July 2010.
[85] Interview with Kristi Tarand, 17 May 2011.
[86] Nagel, op. cit., 86–88.
[87] Ibid., 120.
[88] Karjahärm and Sirk, op. cit., 281.
[89] Ibid., 87, 281.

On 22 March 1983, the ECP CC approved the communist indoctrination plan for young people in school for 1983–1985. A Russian language exam was added to the final exams required for graduation from basic school and secondary school, and a Russian language exam was also required for enrollment in many schools of higher education.[90] At this point ended the "below-the-line" status of Russian, which previously permitted pupils who failed Russian to move on to the next grade, and the Party policy game of pretending as if all pupils were studying Russian voluntarily.[91]

School reform

According to Veronika Nagel, who has researched Estonia's educational policy, school reform began in Estonia with the 1987 teachers' congress, where the teachers' voice was so insistent and urgent that schools practically freed themselves at that point from Moscow's pressure and guidance.[92]

The enactment passed on 19 May 1988 by the Estonian SSR Supreme Soviet Presidium did away with the Estonian SSR Ministry of Education, the Ministry of Higher and Vocational Secondary Education, and the state vocational education committee and formed the Estonian SSR Educational Committee under union republic control.[93] The enactment "Concerning Reorganization of the Central Organizations for Governing the State in the Estonian SSR," passed on 21 December 1989 by the Estonian SSR Supreme Soviet Presidium, did away with the educational committee and established the Ministry of Education.[94] Rein Loik became the Minister of Education.

Beginning with the 1988–1989 academic year, twelve-grade secondary education was restored in Estonian-language general education schools. Secondary school remained at eleven grades in Russian-language general education schools. All eight-grade schools in the republic were turned into nine-grade schools.[95] School attendance was made compulsory for all six- and seven-year-old children, depending on the level of the child's development,

---

[90] ECP CC Bureau directive "Concerning the plan for measures for communist indoctrination of young people in schools 1983–1985," 22 March 1983, ERAF.1.4.6852, 17–21.
[91] Interview with Kalju Luts, 28 June 2011.
[92] Nagel, op. cit., 153.
[93] Eesti NSV Ülemnõukogu Presdiidiumi seadlus Eesti NSV Riikliku Hariduskomitee moodustamise kohta. *ENSV Teataja 1988*, 24, 285.
[94] Eesti NSV Ülemnõukogu Presiidiumi seadlus Eesti NSV riigivalitsemise keskorganite süsteemi ümberkujundamise kohta. *ENSV Teataja 1989*, 40, 625.
[95] Nagel, op. cit., 139.

and lasted until the pupil completed ninth grade or turned sixteen years of age.[96]

A new curriculum was adopted for the 1989–1990 academic year. The study workload was reduced mainly by reducing the number of lessons and the proliferation of facts. The teaching of *kodulugu* (homeland history) was restored in elementary grades. The learning of foreign languages was expanded. The teaching of Russian began in the third grade instead of the first grade. The relative proportion of the sciences was reduced in basic education. Military training was replaced by instruction in national defense, health education, or family studies. Religious studies, which had been prohibited during the Soviet era, also began within the framework of school reform in schools in 1990, at some pupils' request.[97]

The liberation of education from communist ideology in textbook-based content, however, took place gradually because there simply were no new textbooks by that time. In January 1990, forty-four geography teachers wrote an open letter asserting that the old textbooks were unsuitable because they were filled with idealistic sentences like "The Estonian SSR borders on industrially developed republics and oblasts. However, since its neighbors are poor in energy resources, we provide them with electrical energy as well." The first textbooks to be replaced were those for geography, history, and biology.[98]

Results of ideological pressure

Despite all the Soviet regime's efforts, it failed to ideologically re-educate Estonians. According to Kalju Luts, the atmosphere of fear in education disappeared when Arnold Green was minister (1958–1960). Luts said that a great deal depended on the local union republic minister of education and his skill in presenting local conditions in Moscow. Green knew how to do that while at the same time remaining very Estonian-minded.[99]

"Internal" control was used in schools to control the content and ideology of the work of teachers. This meant that in addition to school inspectors and checks by the Party, the school principal and head teacher also visited lessons. Control of the ideological aspect, however, remained mostly on paper.[100] At the same time, all superiors in Soviet society were forced into the role of

---

96   Ibid., 142.
97   Ibid., 151.
98   Ibid.
99   Interview with Kalju Luts, 28 June 2011.
100   Ibid.

supervisors. This means that if a lathe turner said something against the state, the master carpenter was also penalized; if the master carpenter behaved in a non-Soviet way, the shop manager was also penalized. Thus according to historian Lauri Vahtre, the school principal had to penalize a pupil who did something against the state right away and with the strictest penalties, if he did not want to be penalized himself.[101] The alternative was to cover it up, which was also done. In this respect, the author cannot wholly agree with Lauri Vahtre concerning immediate and strict penalization, or with Richard Pipes. The latter claims that the Soviet Union produced people who cared only for themselves because they could not count on anyone else.[102] True, the system did condition people to save themselves at the expense of their fellow human beings on many occasions. Nevertheless, this cannot be taken as the only possible response. Each of the teachers from that time who were interviewed had some story about how someone was denounced and the school leadership hushed the matter up. Pupils play a large role in this as well. English teacher Kristi Tarand recalls that she would never have made it through all the checks conducted in her class unscathed if her pupils had not covered for her. One humorous example is a 1985 incident that happened when Martin Luther's birthday was celebrated in Tarand's lessons. A girl from one of the upper grades was the first to come to class. She had written a paper on the topic, and the school's Party organizer came to listen to her presentation, even though he did not understand English. Later, a boy whom the Party organizer sat beside told Tarand that the Party organizer had asked whether the girl had said that religion was opium for the masses. The boy replied that of course she had, that that was what the presentation began with. The pupils also never reported that the teacher told them stories about the struggle of Estonians for freedom in ancient times, for example, and used ancient national heroes to expand vocabulary and for comparative analysis.[103] Here the pupils did not save their own skins. Instead, it can be said that Soviet conditions created the conditions for denouncing fellow citizens as well as for people to stick together among themselves; which path a person chose depended on the person himself.

Vilma Kahk believes that ideological indoctrination had practically zero effect. She recalls:

---

[101] Vahtre, L. *Absurdi impeerium.* Tartu: Tammerraamat, 2007, 167.

[102] Pipes, op. cit., 85.

[103] Interview with Kristi Tarand, 17 May 2011.

We have discussed with teachers of those days that the ideological pressure that was applied really did intensify in the 1980s, when we started being invited to lectures more frequently and they were held in school as well. But it did not bear results. If the pupil's home was Estonian-minded, even a very loyal Soviet teacher would not have been able to change the pupil. Perhaps that [ideological indoctrination] had an effect on the Russian-speaking contingent, but certainly not even on all of them either. So in my opinion, the results of that ideological work were practically zero.[104]

A statement of communist indoctrination work concerning Tallinn Secondary School No. 21 is preserved in the Tallinn Municipal Archives, which expresses satisfaction that efforts have been made to shift the main emphasis of work in ideological and political indoctrination to subject lessons: "To this end, special plans have been required this year from subject teachers where they indicate the main themes through which they can cultivate Soviet patriotism and proletarian internationalism in pupils."[105] That cultivation never got past the planning stage.

Similarly, longtime teachers of literature and mathematics Sirje and Taavet Kuurberg find that ideological pressure did not succeed in changing anyone's views. A pupil's mentality was just the way he or she brought it from home. Furthermore, ideological indoctrination in school was mostly reduced to showing it on paper. Even those requirements that had to be implemented in reality as well – such as the observance of Soviet holidays – everyone recognized as being only the fulfillment of formal requirements. And whoever participated wholeheartedly in such activities was not conditioned to do so by the ideological indoctrination conducted in school. All the ideological pressure managed to achieve was to prevent sensitive topics from being spoken about. At first, people did not dare to speak, and later on some Estonian historical and cultural events were simply no longer even known among the younger generations. Again, that also depended on the kind of family the pupil came from.[106] Allan Liim, history and social science teacher and principal of Tartu's Secondary School No. 1, also believes the only effect of ideological indoctrination was the emergence of parallel consciousness, meaning that teachers and pupils simply knew when to be silent and, when one spoke, what to say. The fact that all this indoctrination work remained a formality is confirmed by the fact that many of the graduates of Tartu's

---

[104] Interview with Vilma Kahk, 17 May 2010.
[105] Tallinn's N. Gogol Secondary School No. 21, statement concerning communist indoctrination work in the school, 20 October 1972, 5, TLA.R-11.1.176a.
[106] Interview with Sirje and Taavet Kuurberg, 22 July 2010.

A.H. Tammsaare Secondary School No. 1 actively participated in the political life of newly independent Estonia.[107] Historian Jelena Zubkova also claims that just as the harsh Stalinist version of Sovietization was doomed to failure, so was its liberal version. There was no future in trying to make Estonia and the other Baltic countries Soviet. Those three countries remained a problematic region for Moscow until the collapse of the Soviet Union.[108]

The existence of secret youth organizations is further proof of the failure of ideological work. At least eighty-two court cases in 1945–1954 involving anti-Soviet youth groups have been identified. A total of 835 suspects were identified in those cases, of which 657 persons (including seventeen teachers) were put on trial. The offenses of the persons put on trial were mostly repeat offenses. They included distributing flyers; tearing down election posters, slogans, portraits, and flags; hoisting blue, black, and white (Republic of Estonia) flags in public places; and collecting and disseminating prohibited literature. A total of forty-seven groups and organizations also had weapons, which were extremely easy to find in the postwar period.[109]

From 1954 to 1957, the ESSR KGB (Committee for State Security) Fourth Department uncovered nine anti-Soviet organizations with ninety-four members. Another eight youth groups with thirty-eight members were exposed in 1958.[110] Anti-Soviet feelings at times pushed young people to the other extreme, and such youths tended to glorify Nazi Germany. The security organs had to constantly deal with "fascist" attitudes. For instance, a dispatch from the ESSR KGB to the ECP CC in 1986 complained that young people had suddenly started taking an unwholesome interest in fascist symbols and in fascism in general.[111] This was the case even though school textbooks had been preaching for decades about the "misanthropic" nature of fascism and the "humanity," "struggle for peace,"and "friendship among the peoples" of the Soviet regime etc.

Resistance to the regime was also expressed in illegal publications. In 1978–1979, an underground newspaper entitled *Poolpäevaleht* (*Semi-Daily Newspaper*) appeared in Tartu. Seven issues of this paper were published in

---

[107] Allan Liim's letter to Eli Pilve, 27 July 2010.

[108] Zubkova, J. *Baltimaad ja Kreml 1940–1953*. Tallinn: Varrak, 2009, 245, 251.

[109] Josia, U. Poliitilistest kohtuprotsessidest nõukogudevastaste noorteorganisatsioonide ja – gruppide üle ENSV-s aastail 1945–1954. In Josia, U. (ed.). *Saatusekaaslased: Eesti noored vabadusvõitluses 1944–1954*. Tartu, Tallinn: Endiste Õpilasvabadusvõitlejate Liit, 2004, 29–32.

[110] Niitsoo, V. *Vastupanu 1955–1985*, Tartu, 1997, 15, 19.

[111] Справка о причинах и факторах, способствующих возникновению негативных проявлений в молодежной среде ЭССР на базе анализа оперативной обстановки за 1983–1986 годы, ERAF.1.302.499, 7–12.

all, and they circulated primarily among university students and intellectuals in Tartu and Tallinn. This, however, indicates that the ideological teaching received with secondary education was a waste of time in terms of its objective. Holger Kaljulaid, a pupil at Secondary School No. 1 in Kohtla-Järve, issued an underground newspaper all by himself, mostly transcribing forbidden Radio Liberty and Voice of America broadcasts but also publishing original material. He edited and published a total of ten issues of this newspaper, *Isekiri*. The last of these issues appeared in 1985, when the publisher was sent to serve in the Soviet Army. Other similar underground newspapers were issued as well.[112] If we add to this the enthusiasm for the idea of freedom of the time of the Singing Revolution and the actual restoration of independence, sufficient manifestations can be found in the opinion of the author to convince readers of the miscarriage of Soviet ideological indoctrination that, furthermore, was often implemented only on paper, at least in the case of those pupils who were brought up with a different view of the world at home.

Conclusion

The Russian Communist Party program adopted in 1919 demanded that schools bring up a generation that would be able to achieve communism. Whereas changes in Estonian education policies did indeed begin in the first year of the Soviet occupation, the result was still formal and did not change much. The real changes occurred from 1944 to 1953. The most attention was paid to teaching history, literature, geography, and certainly the Estonian and Russian languages. Teachers were expected to praise Soviet peoples and their unity in other classes as well, and the superiority of the Russian nation had to be generally accepted.

Nevertheless, Stalin-era propaganda did not quite achieve what was expected of it. People still remembered well what life had been like in independent Estonia and what happened to them when they were supposed to build communism. Deportation and imprisonment were not stories from the past but everyday events that happened to them and to their nearest and dearest. Ideological pressure was taken as something unavoidable – disliked but to be endured. The new generation that had not lived in the time before the Soviet occupation was not yet of school age. This was the generation that could truly be influenced by propaganda if (!) it were allowed to be spread at home and at school.

---

[112] Pesti, A. "Poolpäevalehe" lugu. *Vikerkaar*, 1990, no. 11, 81–87; Niitsoo, op. cit., 105–108.

Nikita Khrushchev's speech about the personality cult and its consequences led to society's gradual liberation from the oppression of fear. More liberal conditions were expressed among the student body primarily through a reduction in the number of members of the Komsomol and Pioneer youth organizations. Teachers dared to grumble about translated textbooks and to speak up more during classroom lessons on forbidden topics. On 30 June 1956, the CPSU CC Presidium passed the decision "Concerning the Personality Cult and Overcoming Its Consequences," which criticized Stalin's personality cult but stressed that it did not change the socialist nature of Soviet society. The decision's objective was to dampen the effect of Khrushchev's address delivered at the CPSU Twentieth Congress. The release of political prisoners continued in 1956–1957, and some of them were rehabilitated as well. At the same time, independence-mindedness gathered strength in some locations. Under these circumstances, ideological pressure, which had in the meantime relented somewhat, began intensifying again, culminating in the Russification policy of the late 1970s. For a certain period of time, Russification was taken to extremes – even in math lessons, pupils had to be taught the Russian equivalent of every new mathematical term. Pressure increased even further in the 1980s in response to ever more active aspirations towards freedom, but to no avail. Estonians' national feeling was too strong to be uprooted in the space of half a century. According to the memories of contemporaries of that time, all attempts at ideological brainwashing were of no consequence, because if a pupil's home was Estonian-minded, even a very loyal teacher could not manage to re-educate the pupil. The effect of ideological indoctrination lay only in the fact that pupils learned to read between the lines and to carefully choose whom to say what to. The ideological pressure forced on society, however, succeeded in producing patriots of the independent Republic of Estonia, even if only because forbidden fruit is sweeter.

School reform began in Estonia with the 1987 teachers' congress. In 1988, twelve-grade secondary education was restored in Estonian-language general education schools. Secondary school remained at eleven grades in Russian-language general education schools. All eight-grade schools in the republic were converted into nine-grade schools. A new curriculum was adopted in 1989. The workload of pupils was reduced primarily by reducing the number of lessons and the overabundance of facts in the required lesson plan. The learning of foreign languages was expanded and the teaching of Russian began in the third grade instead of the first grade, as was previously the case. The relative proportion of sciences was reduced in basic education. Military training was replaced with courses in national defense and health and family studies. The liberation of the textbook-based content of education from communist ideology, however, took place gradually, because it took time to write new textbooks.

Giving a lesson in history –
Soviet attempts to manipulate Estonian
émigré communities

Simo Mikkonen

In the Soviet Union, memory was a key political arena in which conflicting views were undesired and the official version forcefully consolidated. As Estonia was annexed by the Soviet Union, the most important aspect of memory politics was to reinforce the idea that Estonians had voluntarily entered the Soviet family of peoples. After World War II, the interpretation of the Estonian position during the war became equally crucial. The third such issue in memory politics was in the more general Estonian history – how far national characteristics ought to be manifested along with the general Soviet historiography and culture. The hard task of Estonian historiography in the twentieth century was that the Soviet and Nazi occupations, as well as radical national Estonians, had repeatedly severed the continuity of history-writing. Thus the lack of stable and impartial history made it difficult to defend any line of Estonian history-writing, which significantly contributed to the controversy.[1] Thus when, after World War II, Soviet officials confronted Estonian émigré communities, they sought to prevent rival interpretations of Estonian history from being consolidated. Indeed, Soviet officials paid enormous attention to promoting the Soviet versions of local histories and national identities. The primary objective was to disarm anti-Soviet individuals and isolate them from other émigrés. The secondary objective was to make émigrés more Soviet-minded and prone to accept the Soviet interpretation of their national history. Soviet authorities believed that

---

[1] This controversy and the constant changes in the administration and their impact on his-tory-writing are perhaps best depicted by famous Estonian novelist Jaan Kross, who in se-veral of his novels touches upon the subject. Estonian émigrés naturally depicted the Soviet era as a dreadful occupation in stark comparison to "the golden age" of the 1920s and 1930s. See, e.g., Oras, A. *Baltic Eclipse*. London: V. Gollancz, 1948, in which Ants Oras describes independent Estonia with all the emotion that only a recent exile can: as practically the happiest and most developed place on Earth.

this would reinforce the Soviet version of Estonian history within the Soviet Union as well.

Soviet authorities naturally hid their true motivations for engaging émigrés for most of the Cold War. Émigré work was described as cultural work veiled behind such terms as friendship and mutual understanding. Consequently, the means for reaching Estonian émigrés, as well as the organizations that took care of this work, were numerous. They also changed over time. In the immediate postwar years, the aim was merely to repatriate everyone that the Soviet Union regarded as its citizens, but who were outside its borders at the end of the war – the "displaced persons, "*peremeshchennie litsy.*[2] This work was closely controlled by Moscow and the KGB. The second phase started throughout the 1950s and extended into the late 1960s.[3] At this point, Estonian officials seem to have had much more autonomy over the methods and even organizations handling this work. By the 1970s, however, there was little trace of the former national emphasis. While some of the Soviet activity concerning Estonian émigrés always originated from Soviet Estonia, much of it was Moscow-controlled, and Communist Party organs retained firm control. Even so, Soviet Estonian personnel had a crucial role in contacting Estonian émigrés abroad. Initially, Soviet embassies kept Soviet Estonian officials updated about what was happening among émigrés, but quite early on, the Soviet Embassy in Sweden, had their own Estonian officials, reflecting the importance the high echelons of the Soviet Communist Party placed on this work.

The increased autonomy of Soviet Estonian officials in émigré work from the late 1950s onwards reflected the change in objectives for this work. When it turned out that it was wishful thinking to expect a major influx of émigrés back to the Soviet Union, the initial target of repatriating émigrés was given up. Even so, throughout the Soviet era, Soviet officials remained convinced that émigrés constituted a potential threat that somehow needed to be dealt with.[4] The primary threat was that émigré circles' memories could

---

[2]   Displaced persons and their fates have been described in Salomon, K. *Refugees in the Cold War: Toward a New International Refugee Regime in the Early Postwar Era.* Lund: Lund University Press, 1991; Wyman, M. *DPs: Europe's Displaced Persons, 1945–1951.* Philadelphia: The Balch Institute Press, 1989.

[3]   See e.g. Mikkonen, S. Mass Communications as a Vehicle to Lure Russian Émigrés Homeward. In *Journal of International and Global Studies* (Lindenwood UP) 2, no. 2: April 2011, 45–61. This article discussed the changes in Soviet approach towards people it considered its citizens who were living abroad, meaning exiles, émigrés, and "displaced persons."

[4]   Letter of Stepan Chervonenko from the Ukrainian Communist Party to the Central Committee of the Communist Party, no later than 6.09.1958, RGANI (Russian State Archives of

not be suppressed like in Soviet Estonia, where celebrations, monuments, publications, and official discourse could be kept within the official limits. With help from Western governments, émigrés could potentially spread their version of the Estonian past and culture not only internationally but also within Soviet Estonia, thus endangering the Soviet position.[5] Soviet officials therefore needed to sell their version of Soviet Estonian culture and past to émigré communities. It was a battle for the legitimacy of Soviet rule in Estonia.

With this framework, I try to give a glimpse of how Soviet officials perceived Estonian émigrés throughout the Soviet era and how they attempted to confront them. Instead of émigré publications, the main emphasis is on the Russian-language materials collected mostly in Tallinn and Moscow archives explaining the dynamics between Moscow and Tallinn in regards to émigré affairs. I will deal very little with the KGB, which inarguably was active throughout the period, but whose central archives are not accessible. This article is more interested in the triangle of the Kremlin, Soviet Estonia, and Estonian émigrés – their mutual relationship and especially the Soviet use of soft power towards émigrés.

Repatriating the displaced Soviet citizens

Immediately after the war, the Soviet government's primary objective was to repatriate all the displaced people from Soviet-occupied areas.[6] No other Soviet nation needed as large a percentage of its total population repatriated as Estonians. By the end of the war, there were camp inmates who had fought

---

Recent History) f. 5, op. 33, d. 75, 102–109. The Central Committee had received several letters expressing concerns about the threat posed by anti-Soviet émigrés.

[5]   Operation Rollback during the Truman administration (1945–1952) and the subsequent American attempts to use anti-Soviet émigrés in large-scale operations against the Soviet Union prompted Soviet officials to launch counter-actions. About American work among Soviet émigrés, see Mikkonen, S. Exploiting the Exiles: The Soviet Emigration in US Cold War Strategy. *Journal of Cold War Studies* 14, no. 2 (Spring 2012), 98–127. These American operations gave birth, for example, to Radio Free Europe, as well as contributing to the formation of the Assembly of Captive European Nations.

[6]   There is not much literature on Soviet objectives towards émigrés, but among them, the best is perhaps: Iontsev, V.A., Lebedeva, N.M., Nazarov, M.V., and Okorokov, A.V. (eds.). *Emigratsiya, i Repatriatsiya v Rossii* (Moscow: Popechitelstvo o nuzhdakh Rossiiskikh repatriantov, 2001). On the Baltic case, some enlightening remarks about émigrés and Soviet rule are made in Misiunas, R., and Taagepera, R. *The Baltic States: Years of Dependence 1940–1990.* London: Hurst and Co., 1993, in which they touch upon the role that émigrés had on the development of their native countries under Soviet rule.

in the Red Army and were captured by Germans, those who had fought in the German army, forced and voluntary laborers in the German area, and those who had escaped from Estonia to Sweden in either 1940 or 1944. Although repatriations were indisputably extensive, in this paper, evacuations and forced migration primarily create the context for the postwar operations of Soviet officials.

In the postwar situation, with Europe in ruins, Soviet nationalities were repatriated to the Soviet Union even from Western territories, sometimes by force. The Baltic nations, however, were considered a special case by the West.[7] Thus, while well over 100,000 Estonians were displaced, Soviet officials managed to get only 20 percent of them returned by 1953. In the case of other Soviet nationalities, the amount was close to 95 percent. The majority of those 20,000 who were repatriated were most likely found in the Soviet-occupied areas and Finland, which was forced to sign an agreement on turning over Soviet citizens. But just as with other Soviet citizens, with Estonians the stream of displaced citizens back to their native land turned into a trickle by the end of 1947. In 1952 only twenty-five Estonians were repatriated to Soviet Estonia from outside the Soviet Union through repatriation efforts.[8]

According to official reports about repatriation work in 1953, some 45 percent of repatriated Estonians came from displaced persons camps, and these were typically civilians. These camps were nominally controlled by the United Nations, but political control was with the occupation powers, yet the Soviets seemed to count these as special cases. The remaining repatriates were listed by the countries they returned from, thus almost 40 percent came from Germany (most likely primarily from the Soviet-occupied zones), one-tenth from Finland, and the rest from a number of other countries (for instance, one Estonian from Canada, six from the United States, four from Australia,

---

[7]   See, e.g., Medijainen, E. The USA, Soviet Russia and the Baltic States: From Recognition to the Cold War; and Made, V. The Estonian Government-in-Exile: A Controversial Project of State Continuation. In Hiden, J., Made, V., and Smith, D.J. (eds.). *The Baltic Question during the Cold War*. New York: Routledge, 2009.

[8]   Report about the work of the department of repatriation of CM ESSR for 1945–1953, ERA.R-1970.2.112, 65–82. This document gives yearly details for the repatriation of citizens from the Estonian area. Of 20,671 that were repatriated from 1945 to 1953, 11,170 were civilians and 9,451 soldiers from the German army. Interestingly, Estonian POWs from the Red Army were not mentioned in these lists, or they were categorized as civilians. Overall Soviet figures can be found in GARF (Russian State Archives) f. 9526, op. 3, d. 175 and op. 4, d. 1, 62, 70, 223; also quoted in Zemskov, V.N. "Vtoraia emigratsiia" I otnoshenie k nei rukovodstva SSSR, 1947–1955. *Istoriia rossiiskogo: zarubeznaia emigratsiia iz SSSR-Rossii 1941–2001 gg.* Moscow: Institut rossiiskoi istorii RAN, 2007, 63–91.

twenty-seven from Great Britain, and four from China).[9] At this point, Soviet officials were using mostly diplomatic channels and foreign policy efforts to get foreign governments to turn over Estonians. But they were also using a number of propaganda measures in order to get Estonians abroad to return. Naturally, there was a lot of printed propaganda, but radio also played an important part in reaching émigrés. Although most of the repatriation work was carried out by Soviet officials, this work required a lot of Estonians as well. Before 1953, seventy-three Soviet Estonians had already participated in making radio programs abroad. Also, 282 of those who had returned from abroad contributed to programs. Furthermore, twenty-four collective letters and 2,726 individual letters from Soviet Estonians appealing to Estonians abroad were broadcast. Twice a week an hourlong program in Estonian was broadcast abroad.[10]

The repatriation of Soviet émigrés remained the primary objective throughout the 1950s, even if Soviet officials were facing difficulties with Western governments soon after the war ended. Secret correspondence between the Soviet Embassy and foreign ministries in Moscow and Latvia in 1946 points out that the Soviets were frustrated with Swedish officials. The Swedes subsequently not only declined to hand any Baltic nationals back to the Soviet Union but also denied any information about the existence and composition of such populations on their territory. Soviet security organs, therefore, tried to draw up lists of those presumably in Sweden in order to make it easier to reach them.[11] Thus Soviet officials spent a lot of time determining émigrés' whereabouts in the West, then locating their relatives back in Soviet Estonia and getting these people to write letters appealing to their émigrés relatives, or in other ways contacting them.[12] Naturally, as the register grew, whenever Soviet citizens were sent abroad, the authorities checked whether they had relatives or friends whom they could approach when visiting abroad. Emotions played a big part in Soviet strategy concerning the émigrés in general. Homesickness, worries over relatives or

9   Report about the work of the department of repatriation of CM ESSR for 1945–1953, ERA.R-1970.2.112, 109.

10   Report about the work of the department of repatriation of CM ESSR for 1945–1953, ERA.R-1970.2.112, 83–104.

11   Letter from the Advisor of the Soviet Embassy in Sweden, S. Vazarov, to Deputy Foreign Minister of Latvia, J. Avotins, September 1946. In Plakans, A. *Experiencing Totalitarianism: The Invasion and Occupation of Latvia by the USSR and Nazi Germany 1939–1991*. Bloomington, IN: Author House, 2007, 302–303.

12   Estonian department of repatriation, N. Filatov's letter to Heinsaar, 30 December 1952, ERA.R-1970.2.113, 1.

friends in the Soviet Union, and pride in everything Estonian were blatantly exploited in Soviet propaganda.

From repatriation towards cultural work

In January 1953, shortly before Stalin's death, the first phase of the repatriation work came to an end. The Estonian Foreign Ministry ceded authority over future repatriation work to the Soviet Foreign Ministry and sent its remaining registers to the KGB. The Office for Hunting Economy (sic!) took premises from the Estonian office for repatriation.[13] But Soviet operations concerning émigrés were already proceeding in a new way to counter the threat they felt émigrés posed, even if repatriation still remained the main objective. In 1955 the Soviet Committee on Return to the Homeland (Komitet za vozvrashchenie na rodinu) was established in Berlin. It was the last, and mostly failed, effort at massive repatriation of Soviet citizens. It was responsible for the émigré work at the Soviet level. This committee controlled a sizable propaganda machine distributing magazines and printed materials, but it also boasted its own radio station designed purely for Soviet émigrés. The methods of this committee were softer than its predecessors, which is partly related to the increasing presence of the Soviet Union in the international arena after Stalin's death. The committee also commissioned the aforementioned publishing and broadcasting of letters directed to individual émigrés. The magazine and radio channel were first named *Za vozvrashchenie na rodinu* (*On Return to Homeland*), but were soon changed to the more neutral *Golos Rodinu* (*Voice of the Homeland*). The committee itself became known as the Rodina Association. All this work aimed at émigrés' voluntary repatriation, which I have previously studied in the general Soviet context.[14] But intensification of the work with Estonian émigrés was not far behind. In 1955, an Estonian representative was placed at the Soviet Embassy in Sweden. He was eventually Enno Mikkelsaar, lecturer of political economy at Tartu University.[15]

Reports of the Soviet Foreign Ministry also indicate that the work with émigrés was generally changing towards the late 1950s. Along with describing the composition and actions of Estonian émigrés, new lines of action

---

[13] About terminating Estonian department of repatriation, 1 February1953, ERA.R-1970.2. 113, 62–64.

[14] Mikkonen, S. Mass Communications as a Vehicle to Lure Russian Émigrés Homeward. *Journal of International and Global Studies* 2, no. 2: April 2011, 45–61.

[15] MID's Baranenkov's letter to Müürisepp, 22 September 1955, ERA.R-1970.2.117, 93–95.

were suggested in order to better reach émigré communities. A cultural approach was preferred: attempts were made to increase émigré interest in contemporary Soviet Estonian culture through magazines, movies, artistic tours, and even émigrés' tourist trips to Soviet Estonia. The further marginalization of anti-Soviet émigré organizations was to be combined with this new approach. Anti-Soviet émigrés were to be presented as troublemakers, and Soviet Estonia's good intentions towards émigrés were to be emphasized, to make anti-Soviet émigrés' proclamations look like empty propaganda.[16]

Attempts to promote the official Soviet version of Estonian history held an important position in the cultural work with émigrés in general. Magazines and radio programs to Estonian audiences abroad carefully followed the official line. Naturally, films and documentaries produced in Soviet Estonia that were also brought to émigré audiences via Soviet embassies had gone through Soviet censorship. This new kind of cultural work naturally drained a lot of resources, but it was considered highly important in countering émigrés' anti-Soviet operations. Thus the selling of the official Soviet version of Estonian history became an important part of the Soviet Cold War strategy, something that was believed to sow discord among Estonian émigré communities.[17]

Similarly, by increasing emotional ties between Estonian émigrés and their former native land, all chances to isolate and marginalize political émigré organizations from the majority of émigrés were exploited. For this purpose, select notable émigré artists and scholars were approached and invited to visit their homeland. Such contacts were hoped to serve as bridgeheads through which larger numbers of émigrés would admit the benevolence of the Soviet Union and downplay anti-Soviet attitudes.[18] An early example was Eduard

---

16 For example, ERA.R-1970.2.122 contains considerable correspondence between the Soviet Foreign Ministry, the Embassy in Sweden, and Soviet Estonian officials about émigré work in the late 1950s. The cultural approach and the use of soft power are at the center of these talks. Moscow had urged all the republics to enhance anti-émigré work in spring 1958, especially through special radio broadcasts and printed media. Käbin reported to Moscow about how the work was proceeding in Estonia in October 1958. See About strengthening counter-propaganda, not before 23 October 1958, RGANI f. 5, op. 33, d. 74, 92–95.

17 Käbin's letter to Central Committee CP, 10 April 1959, RGANI f. 5, op. 33, d. 74, 96–99. Käbin was discussing possibilities of increasing radio propaganda to supplement the effectiveness of print media in North America, where Estonian broadcasts could still not be heard.

18 Käbin's letter to Central Committee CP, 18 January 1966, ERAF.1.302.38, 3–4. Käbin presented a request for inviting émigrés to visit Soviet Estonia via Intourist for propaganda purposes. Émigrés would come from Sweden, England, France, and Canada. Control was to be given to the Estonian Friendship Society.

Tubin, an acknowledged Estonian composer from Sweden. Tubin surely had his own motives to be in touch with Soviet Estonia, but Soviet officials wanted to use him for their own ends. He was given a chance to distribute his music in Soviet Estonia and was, for instance, commissioned to write an opera, *Barbara von Tisenhusen*, for the Estonia Theater.[19] He was also used to spread Soviet Estonian music abroad. These kinds of friendly connections were believed by Soviet officials to be poison to anti-Soviet émigrés, who were against any kind of connections with the Soviets.

Increased émigré-related activities in the Soviet Union throughout the 1950s also reflected Estonian governmental structures. In 1960 VEKSA, Väliseestlastega Kultuurisidemete Arendamise Ühing (Association for Developing Cultural Ties with Expatriate Estonians), was established. Its purpose was rather similar to other Soviet organs designed to approach Soviet émigrés during the time.[20] The Soviet-level model organ for VEKSA was likely GKKS, the State Committee for Cultural Ties with Foreign Countries. Despite the links to the KGB, GKKS was much softer in its approach than many of its predecessors and successors were.[21] GKKS took its authority from the Ministry of Foreign Affairs; VOKS, which was terminated in 1957; the Radio Committee; and other central organs. GKKS practically created Soviet cultural diplomacy during the Khrushchev era. In this sense, VEKSA's establishment seems to have drawn from the same source of reform within the Soviet administration that gave birth to GKKS. I have not personally studied VEKSA well enough to judge its methods, but apparently it is connected to developments at the Soviet level. Naturally, VEKSA, too, maintained close ties with the KGB, which had the best register of Estonian émigrés. Thus, as Sweden was the most important target area, the first KGB representative in VEKSA, Randar Hiir, would often travel to Sweden to meet and arrange work with Estonian émigrés there.[22]

---

[19] Käbin's memorandum to Central Committee CP about friendly ties between Estonia and foreign countries, 10 March 1969, ERAF.1.302.98, 16.
[20] According to Vasiliy Mitrokhin's KGB lexicon, organizations similar to VEKSA were established in Ukraine and Byelorussia. See Mitrokhin, V. (ed.). *KGB Lexicon: The Soviet Intelligence Officer's Handbook.* Portland, OR: Frank Cass, 267.
[21] The only English-language article to date that discusses GKKS in more detail is Gould-Davies, N. The Logic of Soviet Cultural Diplomacy. *Diplomatic History* 27, no. 2 (April 2003), 193–214. For more in detail in Finnish, see: Mikkonen, S. Neuvostoliiton kulttuurivaihto-ohjelmat – kulttuurista kylmäsotaa vai diplomatiaa? *Historiallinen aikakauskirja* (Finnish Historical Journal), 4/2011.
[22] Decision of Central Committee ECP about Randar Hiir's trip to Sweden, 15 November 1963, ERAF.1.5.88, 1–2. Randar was given 220 rubles for expenses.

But perhaps the most apparent manifestation of Soviet officials' new courage was to invite Estonian émigrés to Soviet Estonia. What better way to point out Soviet achievements than to have émigrés see them with their own eyes and testify to them? They could then publicize the greatness of Soviet Estonia, also emphasized by Khrushchev, who said Estonia was better off with the Soviet Union than it would have been independently.[23] In order to publicize opportunities to travel to Soviet Estonia, officials tried to find representatives of cultural intelligentsia abroad, such as Tubin, who were curious or amicable enough to make the trip. Thus, throughout the 1960s, numerous émigré intellectuals were invited and welcomed to Soviet Estonia, especially in connection with song festivals.[24] Émigré visits in the 1960s typically took place in groups ranging from ten to fifty people at a time. The typical duration of visits seems to have been around ten days. Especially at first, the Estonian Communist Party compiled lists of those to be invited. In addition to Sweden, émigrés arrived from Canada, the United States, and Britain. Apart from visits by cultural luminaries, Estonian officials even wished to organize visits by émigré children to summer camps, like the one in Valkla.[25]

State of the Estonian émigré community according to Soviet officials

As has already been suggested, the Estonian emigration was considered a threat due its uncontrolled collective memory of the Estonian past and resulting interpretation of the present. The threat was upheld and even fueled, at least in part, by Estonian communists. Party Secretary Johannes Käbin outlined the significance of the Estonian émigré community in a November 1966 letter to Soviet Foreign Minister Andrei Gromyko and declared the need to expand Soviet countermeasures. Thus he used the émigré question to expand the authority of Soviet Estonian organs. He was primarily discussing the emigration in Sweden, which in his words was "organized into a number

---

[23] In connection with a state visit to Sweden, Khrushchev had addressed Baltic exiles in an official dinner (apparently aggravated by their anti-Soviet protests during his visit) by giving a lecture about the state of Baltic nations and how they were thriving because of the Soviet Union. See Wiskari, W. Khrushchev Says Baltic Exiles Err. *New York Times*, 24 June 1964, 2.

[24] Käbin's memorandum to Central Committee CP about about friendly ties between Estonia and foreign countries, 10 March 1969, ERAF.1.302.98, 16.

[25] Käbin's memorandum about inviting foreign Estonians to ESSR, 16 June 1966, ERAF.1.302.38, 31–33.

of societies, committees, corporations and such. Some of these were political and professed anti-Soviet actions, and some had a strong influence on the Swedish government." Émigrés in Sweden were also said to distribute propaganda in Estonian, Swedish, English, and German languages in some twenty different newspapers and journals. Käbin believed that while Estonian émigrés were countered through many measures, Soviet Estonia did not have the resources to reach the Swedish people who were influenced by émigré propaganda. Käbin called for concerted efforts with a number of central organizations in Moscow.[26] But actions taken also illustrate that since the Estonian Foreign Ministry and VEKSA were rather small, they aimed at using all-Estonian organs with foreign connections, like the Estonian section of the Soviet-Sweden Friendship Association, to reach émigrés. This was illustrated in cases that in the West were normal cultural exchange, and even for Soviet professionals were part of their normal duty. Indeed, Leida Loone, an Estonian historian, was sent to organize an exhibition of Estonian books to the Royal Library in Stockholm in early spring 1967 as part of the Soviet-Swedish cultural exchanges. From the point of view of the ECP, however, the exhibition was a response to an émigré effort a year earlier displaying 297 émigré publications in the same library.[27]

While Soviet officials feared that Estonian émigrés would manage to worsen Soviet relations with Sweden, it was also believed that émigrés might affect neighboring Finns. According to the Estonian Communist Party, Estonian émigrés had repeatedly approached Finnish tourists to Sweden. For Soviet officials, good relations with Finland and an amicable attitude of Finns towards the Soviet Union were important. Thus, according to Soviet officials, émigrés' work with Finns and attempts to present their view of history and life in Soviet Estonia severely distorted the facts.[28]

But in order to have an effect on émigrés, the Soviets needed accurate information about them. Information was continuously collected, updated, and outlined in a number of reports. The Soviets estimated the total number of Estonians abroad at 80,000, one-quarter of whom lived in Sweden. Estonians were among the most numerous Soviet émigré groupings, if Estonia is treated as a part of the Soviet Union continuously from 1940 onwards. Interestingly, it was indicated that two-thirds of émigrés in Sweden were Swedish subjects (the word "citizen" was not used). Some were mentioned as refusing to give up their Estonian citizenship, like composer Eduard

---

[26] Letter of J. Käbin to MID Gromyko, 15 November 1966, ERAF.1.302.38, 92–93.
[27] A. Vader's report to CC, 2 December 1966, ERAF.1.302.38, 124.
[28] Section of foreign ties of Central Committee ECP, 6 January 1972, ERAF.1.46.471, 1.

Tubin.[29] The Soviet Embassy in Sweden counted 32,000 Soviet citizens in the country in 1961. This included 20,000 Estonians and 6,000 ethnic Swedes from Estonia. Latvians numbered 5,000, while the remaining 1,000 were Lithuanians, Russians, and others. The majority of émigrés were factory workers; very few lived in the countryside. Half of the émigrés lived either in Stockholm or Göteborg. One ball-bearing factory in Göteborg employed over 1,000 Soviet émigrés.[30] These numbers created the framework for intensive work in Sweden. Unlike in many other cases, émigrés were not spread all around but were concentrated in a few major urban areas. This made it easier for Soviets to reach émigré communities.

A 1958 annual report from the Soviet Embassy in Sweden about Estonian émigrés is telling in many respects. It points out that the Soviets believed the wealthier segment of the emigration was hostile to the USSR and was influencing right-wing Swedes, increasing anti-Soviet attitudes. The émigré intelligentsia, in turn, was considered to include people who were interested in Soviet science and arts. The report also mentioned that anti-Soviet émigrés managed to spread fear and negative attitudes towards conditions in Soviet Estonia. It was also mentioned that the magazine for émigrés had changed its name from *Return to the Homeland* to simply *Homeland* (*Kodumaa*), as the former name had elicited furious criticism from some émigrés.[31] Furthermore, according to Soviet officials, even if the number of anti-Soviet émigrés was small, they managed to sabotage many features of the work with émigrés. For instance, a movie club that showed Soviet films received an audience of ten people. In order to calm fears of Soviet Estonia, the embassy's Estonian staff also toured local émigré homes and told them about the embassy's work and various events. Additional visits to Soviet Estonia were also recommended, as émigrés were said to have asked a lot about this.[32]

Germany also harbored a number of Estonian émigrés. An annual report from the Soviet Embassy in West Germany in 1959 estimated that 3,000

---

29 Report on the Estonian emigration in Sweden, 6 June 1959, ERA.R-1970.2.122, 102–116. MID's head B. Podtserov writes to Müürisepp on 22 September 1959.

30 Excerpts from the report from the Soviet Embassy in Sweden about the work of the Consular Department in 1961, ERA.R-1970.2.134, 2–11.

31 Excerpts from the report from the Soviet Embassy in Sweden about the work of the Consular Department in 1958, ERA.R-1970.2.122, 37–42. This report mentioned that many émigrés returned the publications they received to consulates and the embassy, and that famous émigré writer Valev Uibopuu had threatened to start a vicious anti-Soviet campaign in the Swedish press if the embassy did not stop sending him materials.

32 Excerpts from the report from the Soviet Embassy in Sweden about the work of the Consular Department in 1958, ERA.R-1970.2.122, 37–42.

Estonians in Germany (out of a total of 4,000–5,000) were anti-Soviet by nature, and those were based mainly in Munich, Augsburg, Hamburg, and Stuttgart.[33] A significant number of them had served in the Waffen-SS or other such organizations. Some societies of Estonian émigrés were said to be receiving U.S. funding. A few were said to have ties to the American military, and the Soviets worriedly remarked that Americans had an Estonian military section to be used against the Soviet Union in the case of war.[34] It seems that compared to Sweden, or later North America, Estonian émigrés in Germany received little attention, at least in the cultural form. The KGB likely kept a close eye on émigré organizations, but this was not a concern primarily of Soviet Estonia but rather of Moscow. Soviet officials seem to have believed that émigrés in Sweden would be more influenced by cultural work. Also, the emigrant community in Germany was spread out, making it harder to contact them directly.[35]

While Europe (and Sweden in particular) remained in the center of the work well into the 1960s, Canada was slowly turning into an area of important Estonian emigration, and one that grew in importance during the Brezhnev era. In 1962 Soviet Estonian officials demanded resources to reach the émigré community in Canada, whose size was estimated at 17,000 (including 10,000 in Toronto) and growing quickly. This group was also considered to be very active, and yet, it was lamented, the embassy in Canada was working without an Estonian representative. Soviet Estonian officials likely took action due to the attention Canadian Prime John Minister Diefenbaker was giving Estonian affairs. Diefenbaker had received an émigré petition in 1962 urging him to take the Estonian case to the United Nations. The UN was indeed a problem for the Soviet Union and the forum in which Baltic émigrés managed to put forth their view of their native lands. In order to counter the émigré version of the Estonian situation, Soviet officials increased the circulation of *Kodumaa* and *Tõe hääl* (*The Voice of Truth*). Controlling the image of Soviet Estonia was the primary objective of Soviet Estonian officials. Soviet officials also noted that close to 100 Soviet Estonians (sic) had joined their relatives in Canada between 1960 and 1962, and these people were believed to be loyal to the Soviet Union and strongly inoculated against anti-Soviet émigré propaganda.

---

[33]   Excerpts from the report about anti-Soviet actions in West Germany, 23 November 1959, ERA.R-1970.2.122, 65–67.

[34]   Report of the activities of the Estonian emigration in West Germany, 3 April 1961, ERA.R-1970.2.129, 4–10.

[35]   Letter from N. Lunkov (head of MIDs Scandinavian section) to F.T. Gusev at the embassy in Stockholm, 25 November 1959, ERA.R-1970.2.122, 68–69.

Yet Soviet officials felt threatened by the way Estonian émigrés in Canada were celebrating Estonian cultural heritage and commemorating Estonian history. Although this was seemingly innocent and apolitical for many of the participants, it contradicted the official Soviet line about Estonia.[36]

New rise of the émigrés

Canada would become an even bigger headache for Soviet officials in the years to come. Throughout the 1950s and 1960s, émigrés had become active in cultural work and emphasized their Estonian national heritage in their work. Käbin seems to have grasped this threat and actively approached the Central Committee in Moscow about sending Soviet Estonians to counter the supposed threat the North American groups posed. For example, in 1967 there was to be a high-profile World Expo in Montreal. Käbin requested that fifteen Estonians be sent to this event and wanted to include Toronto, the center of Estonian emigration in Canada, in their itinerary. The Expo itself already employed some Soviet Estonians, as the Soviets had heavily invested in their pavilion, making it the most visited pavilion of the whole Expo. Yet Käbin sought to use the occasion to promote Soviet Estonia and counter the efforts of the Estonian emigration in North America.

By the early 1970s, the activities of the Estonian emigration rose to a new level. It seems that a new generation of émigrés had taken up anti-Soviet activities, and once again the Estonian Communist Party felt threatened. Émigrés' work in relation with OSCE, the Organization for Security and Cooperation in Europe, raised special concerns, but Soviets were also increasingly concerned about cultural festivals in North America. Indeed, the first Estonian World Festival in Toronto in 1972 was a major show of émigré unity and, as such, highly alarming to the Soviets. Furthermore, émigrés had been able to get their articles published in the Finnish media.[37] However, the primary attention now turned from Sweden to North America, which had attracted the largest concentration of Estonian émigrés.

The Estonian Communist Party worriedly followed the preparations for the First Estonian World Festival in Toronto in 1972, but it could do little about it. Soviet Estonian officials anticipated that about 15,000 to 20,000 Estonians from all continents would participate in the Festival. For

---

36 Report about the Estonian emigration in Canada, 7 July 1962, ERA.R-1970.2.134, 29–37.
37 Department of foreign relations of the Central Committee ECP, 6 January 1972, ERAF.1.46.471, 1–3.

the organizers, the purpose of the festival was to unite Estonian émigrés, make them known to the world, and possibly step up "anti-Soviet actions". Therefore, Soviet Estonian officials prepared countermeasures as much as a year in advance. Yet measures were rather familiar and mild, ranging from displays of amenable émigré artists in Soviet Estonia to the distribution of propaganda materials among émigrés. A book called *The Estonian State and People in the Second World War* was among those to be distributed. Furthermore, new issues of *Kodumaa* magazine, presenting life in Soviet Estonia, were to be distributed heavily. Some Estonian émigrés were also invited to visit Soviet Estonia in an attempt to further isolate anti-Soviet émigrés from the supposedly apolitical majority.[38] There was hardly anything new in these measures. But this was not all. Direct action was planned for Toronto in particular.

Toronto, which had become a major center for Estonian emigration and thus would host the 1972 festivities, was to be bombarded by photograph collections, literature, and music recordings introducing present-day Soviet Estonia. The Soviet Embassy in Canada also appealed to the mayor of Toronto, the minister of immigration, and the Provincial Secretary of Ontario to abstain from participating in the Estonian festival. But Soviet officials did not forget Sweden, from which numerous Estonian émigrés were expected to travel to the Toronto festival. Therefore, the Estonian Chamber Choir and a ballet group of the Estonia Theater were scheduled for a tour in Sweden. Friendly ties were also to be improved by inviting a basketball team from Stockholm consisting of Estonian émigrés' children to visit Tallinn and play against a team of local schoolchildren.[39] Although some of the efforts might seem irrelevant or even banal, they underline how important Soviet officials considered it to get Estonian émigrés to recognize Soviet rule over Estonia. The Estonian Festival in Toronto, they believed, was going to stress the Soviet occupation of Estonia as well as an émigré interpretation of the Estonian history and heritage. This was taken as a direct challenge to the legitimacy of Soviet Estonia.

Inviting people to Soviet Estonia seems to have been one of the primary ways to create friendly ties with émigrés; it was hoped that they would thus become more amenable to Soviet rule. Indeed, towards the 1970s, it seems as if all émigrés who seemed interested in Soviet Estonia – especially if they were

---

[38] Report on actions prepared by VEKSA against "Estonian World Festival," not before 16 June 1971, ERAF.1.46.471, 4–7.
[39] Ibid.

considered amicable towards it – were potential invitees to Soviet Estonia.[40] Yet while Estonian officials hailed émigré visits as important, the KGB had a key role in letting émigrés into the country. While the KGB stated in 1961, during the Thaw, that émigrés could enter the country, there were still strict limits on where in Estonia they could travel.[41] In practice it was very hard to go beyond Tallinn and other urban areas. This undermined the propaganda value of such trips.

Still, visits by émigré intelligentsia were considered important events to be publicized abroad. Thus, after Eduard Tubin visited Soviet Estonia, the Communist Party rejoiced that on his return to Sweden, he was interviewed by Swedish TV and there praised the musical life of Soviet Estonia. Furthermore, visits by other Estonian émigrés were mentioned in connection with actions against anti-Soviet émigrés. In general, Estonian officials estimated that about one-third of émigrés were loyal to or amenable to the existence of Soviet Estonia. These people were considered most likely to be affected by cultural connections. Even anti-Soviet émigrés were now divided into two categories: hostile, and those with whom negotiation was possible.[42]

Decline of the Soviet Estonian émigré connections

The unlikely benefactors of the Soviet émigré-related operations were Soviet Estonian and émigré intellectuals. While Soviet officials sought to exploit Soviet Estonian intellectuals to influence émigré communities, for many participants this provided a highly coveted chance to go abroad and be in touch with émigré communities, something that the Soviet authorities otherwise considered highly undesirable. Yet during the heyday of cultural operations, in the 1960s, such connections seem to have been surprisingly commonplace. Soon after, however, the Estonian phase in the work with émigrés started to decline, most likely because of the Central Committee's concerns. Perhaps the increasing connections were too much for the KGB, which was quickly strengthening its grip under Brezhnev. At the very least, the national orientation in the émigré work was obviously in trouble: émigré-related reports of the Estonian Communist Party ceased to highlight

---

[40] Letter from Soviet ambassador to Sweden M. Yakovlev to A. Green, 18 February 1974, ERAF 1.46.473, 1.

[41] Letter from vice-chair of Soviet Estonian KGB F. Lätte to Müürisepp, 5 May 1961, ERA.R-1970.2.129, 11.

[42] Excerpts from the report from the Soviet Embassy in Sweden about the work of the consular department in 1961, ERA.R-1970.2.134, 2–11.

Estonians by the 1970s. Instead, reports started to use "the Soviet Union" where Soviet Estonia was mentioned earlier. Thus Estonian national features vanished, and the center was vacated by the Soviet semblances by the 1970s. While Soviet Estonia and its achievements had previously been at the core, now it was the Soviet Communist Party, Soviet nationalities, Soviet foreign policy, and Brezhnev's peace program.[43] In this new rhetoric, the previous flexibility was just a memory. The work itself, however, remained on a familiar path. According to a 1974 report on the work, *Kodumaa* magazine had been sent to 3,751 émigrés, a record number of Estonian émigrés had visited Soviet Estonia, and song festivals were used to increase patriotism and affection towards Soviet Estonia.[44] Yet the new generation of émigrés had become politically active, conditions in Soviet Estonia were not getting better, and politically Moscow was clamping down on Estonian communists. This made unofficial contacts between Estonian émigrés and Soviet Estonians even more important, especially towards the 1980s. Paradoxically, many of these contacts were made possible due to VEKSA's and other organs' cultural operations.

Interestingly, historian Vahur Made has pointed out, the 1960s were a quiet period for the Baltic question on the international scene.[45] This seems to follow the period when Soviets used mostly soft power towards émigrés, when links between Soviet Estonia and émigré communities were nurtured; émigrés were invited to visit their native land; and émigré-related measures generally originated primarily from Soviet Estonia, not Moscow. Whether or not this was a sign that Soviet officials' work had succeeded, during this period émigré-related work was most active, but also fresh. Furthermore, during this period Soviet Estonian officials were also given the most space to maneuver and manage the work. In the 1970s, when Estonia and the Baltic question returned to international politics, Soviet émigré-related work was once again tightly controlled by Moscow, and national characteristics were suppressed in a Soviet-centered agenda. In the 1980s, as is known, the Baltic question once again became topical and received much international attention.

---

[43] Ties between Finland and Soviet Estonia, for example, which had become increasingly active throughout the 1960s, faced some new restrictions. While official connections were encouraged by the Communist Party in the 1960s, in 1970 there was a sudden announcement that connections were ballooning too quickly and that there ought to be tighter control over delegations to Finland. See, e.g., About plans for friendly ties with foreign countries for 1970, 12 March 1970, ERAF 1.9.210, 3.

[44] Report about VEKSA's activities in 1974, ERAF 1.46.473, 7–17.

[45] Made, V. The Baltic Issue during the Cold War. In *Estonian Foreign Policy at the Cross-Roads*, Helsinki: Kikimora Publications, 2002, 113–129.

Yet it is important to remember that throughout the Cold War, the Soviet Union considered émigrés a threat. Ever since World War II, the Soviet relationship with them was at best uneasy. Soviet officials were certain about émigrés' potentially destructive influence on Soviet international propaganda efforts. What was even more threatening was that émigrés actively challenged the Soviet version of Estonian history and questioned the legitimacy of Soviet rule in Estonia. Therefore, even if émigrés were engaged in cultural work and all kinds of soft measures were directed to them, in Soviet propaganda, émigrés were constantly attacked and their credibility questioned. Émigrés were demonized, often in terms of the Soviet version of the history of World War II. Although the émigré community included collaborators, fascists, former SS men, and even some actual war criminals, such individuals were always a small minority. Yet Soviet propaganda depicted politically active émigrés practically as Nazis, heinous war criminals who received their paychecks from American imperialists and warmongers. The propaganda directed to both foreign and domestic audiences questioned how anyone in the Soviet Union could trust such scoundrels. Thus the Soviet approach towards émigrés was always paradoxical: calling on them for co-operation while simultaneously denouncing them. This was due in part to the fact that Soviets never sought to understand émigrés but only to disarm them.[46]

Émigré memories of the golden 1920s and 1930s had to be suppressed. Any unfavorable comparisons between Soviet Estonia and independent Estonia were poison to Soviet officials. The years of independence were officially regarded as times of bourgeois repression of average Estonians, of economic hardship from which the Soviet Union finally freed Estonia. While deviations from the official line could be suppressed in public within the Soviet Union, this was not the case with the émigré community. The Soviets dealt with that community with hard measures, mostly through the KGB. But after the mid-1950s they increasingly used the soft measures described in this article, consisting mostly of propaganda and cultural operations.

---

[46] For example, the fates of those accused of Nazi-related crimes were highly interesting in the eyes of Soviet officials, as they were useful for sowing discord among émigré communities. See, e.g., the case of Aleksander Laak: About the suicide of criminal Aleksander Laak in Canada, ERA.R-1970.2.129, 1–2. Soviet Estonian officials asked for and received information from the Canadian Embassy and Moscow concerning Laak's suicide after his crimes in Estonia during Nazi rule were exposed. Similarly, the former rector of Tartu University, Edgar Kant, who in 1962 was a famed professor at the University of Lund, was, in a secret memorandum, linked to collaboration with the Nazi occupation and to crimes committed in Tartu during that time. See Letter of A. Green to Soviet Foreign Minister A. Gromyko, 28 April 1962, ERA.R-1970.2.134, 18–23.

As far as individual émigrés (or Soviet Estonians) are concerned, getting in touch with Soviet Estonia was, for many of them, hardly a political act. They had reasons ranging from curiosity to family ties to a professional agenda that encouraged them to find connections on the other side of the Iron Curtain. Although the topic goes beyond the scope of this article, it seems highly likely that transnational, people-to-people relations with émigrés grew in importance from the 1970s onwards. In the 1950s and 1960s, Soviets selected mostly highly politically reliable people to be in touch with émigrés, and actions were controlled in many respects. By the 1970s, however, even if the autonomy of Soviet Estonian communists was being questioned, the foreign connections of Estonian citizens were growing. An increasing number of people had personal or professional contacts abroad. Similarly, the younger generation of Estonian émigrés was not as interested in politics as it was in the culture of its motherland. This is not to say that culture did not play a highly important role in the national movement of Soviet Estonia during the 1980s but only that traditional émigré politics were waning in the face of other issues. This, needless to say, calls for the attention of future studies.

Soviet propaganda targeting the Estonian Diaspora

Ivo Juurvee

In the autumn of 1944, over 70,000 Estonians fled from Estonia to Sweden and Germany ahead of the advancing Red Army. Many of these refugees later settled down in other Western countries. This emigration was primarily an economic problem for the Soviet Union, since the expatriates' education, skills, and labor could not be drawn upon during postwar reconstruction. The political problem this emigration presented grew in importance as the Cold War developed. The expatriates' departure en masse convincingly demonstrated to the public abroad, as well as to the residents of Soviet Estonia, that if given a choice, many people would flee the Soviet Union. These problems were addressed through political means and propaganda by forcing or luring refugees back to Estonia. In the late 1950s, however, it became clear that accomplishing this goal was impossible (see Simo Mikkonen's article). The nature of propaganda changed as well. This article focuses on printed Soviet propaganda aimed at expatriate Estonians from the end of the 1950s onward, with a particular focus on Andrus Roolaht, the ESSR's most prominent propagandist working to influence Estonians abroad, and on the KGB's role in directing him, as well as on the treatment of history in his works.

The aims and target groups of Soviet propaganda were comprehensive, yet the author of the printed matter aimed at the small target group of expatriate Estonians was usually one and the same person – Andrus Roolaht (1914–2004; he went by the name Otto Roser until 1938), although he wrote under various pseudonyms. He studied at the Hugo Treffner Upper Secondary School and at Tartu University. In 1938 he went to work at the National Propaganda Office, where he worked until the occupation of Estonia in the summer of 1940. He participated in World War II in the Red Army, serving as a staff clerk. After he was discharged, he worked as a journalist and was employed by the magazine *Pilt ja Sõna* (*Picture and Word*)[1] from 1951 to 1958. Even though Roolaht did not earn a university diploma and the description of his education remained "incomplete higher," he undoubtedly acquired a broad-based education and wide experience and knowledge. Additionally, he gained a great deal of experience in journalism. Roolaht's skill in writing interestingly and eloquently was indisputable.[2]

Roolaht got a job in November 1958 at a newspaper named *Kodumaa* (*Homeland*) that had just begun publication. He remained one of the most important employees for producing propaganda aimed at expatriate Estonians until he retired in 1989. This newspaper was founded at the suggestion of the KGB. This will be considered further below. Unfortunately, it is not known to what extent the KGB intervened in the everyday work of the newspaper's editorial office or if the "organs" already had direct connections to Roolaht at that time.

The editorial office gave Andrus Roolaht's work a positive appraisal. The following was written in the character assessment he was given in 1967: "Comrade Roolaht is a politically developed person with a wide range of experience and knowledge. He has a great deal of experience as a journalist and is a conscientious employee. Comrade Roolaht is very familiar with work among emigrants and applies it in the everyday work of *Kodumaa's* editorial office. He has penned a number of articles exposing the upper crust of the emigrants, which have contributed significantly to splits in emigrant organizations."[3] He was recognized by the state after four years of work at *Kodumaa*. Roolaht was presented with an ESSR Supreme Soviet Presidium certificate of merit in May 1962.[4]

Roolaht was an active member of the Väliseestlastega Kultuurisidemete Arendamise Ühing (Association for Developing Cultural Ties with Expatriate Estonians, known as VEKSA)[5] since its founding in 1960. He also studied at the Theology Institute in the late 1960s. Unfortunately, sources have not

---

[1]   Andrus Roolaht's application forms for permission to travel abroad submitted to the KGB: ERAF.136SM.1.2934, 2, 8, 9, 17, 32; see also Roolaht, A. *Nii see oli... Kroonika ühest unustuseliiva maetud ajastust.* Tallinn: Perioodika, 1990.

[2]   For further information about Roolaht's education, see Juurvee, I. Idabloki eriteenistused Külma sõja ajaloorindel Andrus Roolahe ja Julius Maderi näitel (Special services of the Eastern Bloc on the Cold War's historical front according to the examples of Andrus Roolaht and Julius Mader). *Ajalooline Ajakiri* 1 no. 2 (2009), 51–53.

[3]   Character assessment-recommendation, 30 March 1967: ERAF.136SM.1.2934, 3–4.

[4]   Roolaht's foreign travel form, 15 May 1980: ERAF.136SM.1.2934, 41p.

[5]   In 1976 it was renamed the Society for Developing Cultural Ties with Expatriate Estonians. Its activity was terminated in 1990. The responsible secretary or deputy chairman of the society was always an officer of the ESSR KGB intelligence department.

yet been found that would clarify whether it was the thirst for knowledge or the interests of the KGB that motivated his studies. Roolaht joined the Communist Party in 1971.

Roolaht took a job in the Special Repository Department sector that was being formed at the ESSR Academy of Sciences Academic Library in 1973.[6] All literature and periodicals written and published by Estonian expatriates that arrived in the Estonian SSR were deposited in this sector. The sources of material for these collections were the Estonian Communist Party Central Committee (hereinafter referred to as the ECP CC) Foreign Relations Department; GLAVLIT;[7] the ESSR KGB; Soviet embassies abroad; second-hand bookshops, and book exchanges with other libraries. Furthermore, a significant number of books were confiscated from postal packages sent to Estonia. The received materials were catalogued, and their content was thoroughly examined. The reason for this work was the need to answer inquiries from state and Party institutions concerning the content of literature and newspapers. Printed matter was kept behind three iron doors, according to regulations, and the doors were sealed every evening. Guards were also posted around the clock in the foyer and stairwells of the library. Researchers were permitted access to this collection only if they possessed the required authorized permit, which was not, of course, granted to everybody. Roolaht had two long-serving subordinates in the sector – Lydia Samuseva and Lili-Ann Sinijärv. The *Bülletään* (*Bulletin*), reflecting the content of emigrant literature, was drawn up in triplicate for official purposes six times a year.[8] Surveys of how specific events were reported in expatriate literature were also composed. Thus the sector was important for keeping track of the actions of expatriates – this, among other things, in the interests of the KGB – and in building up propaganda against them.

This position gave Roolaht such a broad overview of expatriate literature and journalism that he was much better informed than most about expatriate Estonians. His day-to-day work left him enough spare time to prepare propaganda publications on historical themes intended for expatriate Estonians, published under the name of Rein Kordes. Roolaht ran the sector until his

---

6   Roolaht's foreign travel file: ERAF.136SM.1.2934.

7   GLAVLIT (Glavnoe upravlenie po okhrane gosudarstvennykh taĭn v pechati) was the Main Administration for Protecting State Secrets in Printed Matter operating under the USSR Council of Ministers, the institution responsible for censorship in the Soviet Union.

8   A. Roolaht's statement concerning the work of the sector in 1983. Rough draft: University of Tallinn Academic Library Center for Expatriate Estonian Literature (hereinafter referred to as TLÜ TR VEKK). These materials have been found recently and are not numbered. I thank Anne Valmas for her help in familiarizing me with them.

retirement in the summer of 1988. The entire collection was opened to researchers without restrictions at the end of the same year.[9]

Roolaht was without question an erudite, skilled writer with a broad range of knowledge and experience. He had some resentment towards the Republic of Estonia in his writings, which could have been conditioned by the financial hardship he experienced in his youth. Roolaht traveled extensively and on both sides of the Iron Curtain, unlike ordinary Soviet citizens. Even before the war, he had been to Finland repeatedly. Between 1965 and 1973, he went to Finland six times and to Sweden once. He also traveled in Poland, Czechoslovakia, and East Germany.[10] Thus he was able to compare political and economic conditions of occupied Estonia to democratic and rather prosperous Finland and Sweden; he also had a good overview of socialist reality in Eastern Europe. Assuming that Roolaht was an intelligent person, it must have required a great deal of willpower for him to continue to believe the in economic superiority of the socialist camp after his travel experiences.

His memoirs were published in 1990, the first and last work written under the name of Andrus Roolaht.[11] He completed the manuscript while he was still working at the library. He later stopped publishing, with the exception of a series of articles published, again under the pseudonym Rein Kordes, in the newspaper *Kesknädal* (*Midweek*) in 2001, where his style is completely recognizable.[12] Andrus Roolaht died in 2004.

The archival material relating to Roolaht's connection to the KGB is scarce. Yet there had to be a connection, because Roolaht's applications for permission to travel to Sweden (including to visit Voldemar Kures, his former colleague from his days before the war at the Propaganda Office, whom the KGB suspected of connections with British intelligence since 1955 at the latest)[13] and Finland were always approved, and those approvals referred to the KGB intelligence department's interest in these trips.[14] We can only agree with Indrek Jürjo in terms of appraisal as well as archival evidence. Yet five years after the publication of his book, Andrus Roolaht himself spoke out on

9   Concerning the collection of expatriate Estonian literature and its opening, see Valmas, A. *Raamatumõtted*. Tallinn: Teaduste Akadeemia Kirjastus, 2006, 47–51.

10 Roolaht's foreign travel file: ERAF.136SM.1.2934.

11 Roolaht, *Nii see oli....*

12 Kordes, R. *Sahinad ajalookoridoris. Kesknädal*, 7–28 November 2001.

13 *Aruanne Riikliku Julgeoleku Komitee 2. Vastuluure osakonna tööst. 1955 aasta* (Report on the Work of the State Security Committee 2nd Counterintelligence Department), Ad Fontes 14. Tallinn: Eesti Riigiarhiivi Filiaal, 1998, 18–19.

14 Jürjo, I. *Pagulus ja Nõukogude Eesti: vaateid KGB, EKP ja VEKSA arhiividokumentide põhjal.* Tallinn: Umara, 1996, 229–230.

the same topic – again under the name of Rein Kordes. He identified KGB officer Vsevolod Naidjonkov as his "stagnation-era curator."[15] In a 2002 interview, Roolaht replied to a journalist's question concerning the extent to which the KGB checked up on his work: "It didn't check up on me at all. I did what they wanted me to do. I was a very close acquaintance of the head of the KGB, General August Pork.[16] [...] Thanks to him, I got to go abroad as much as I wanted to and naturally, always at their expense." Roolaht added, "I was very highly thought of. I even got money in an envelope twice a year." He repeats that Naidjonkov supervised his propaganda work.[17]

It can be added to what has been written above that the sector of the ESSR Academy of Sciences library headed by Roolaht operated primarily in the interests of the KGB, and the same applied to VEKSA as well.

Andrus Roolaht (the furthest behind the table) at the VEKSA meeting, 1965

---

[15] Kordes, op. cit.
[16] It is difficult to say whether they really were "very close," but presumably they were acquaintances.
[17] Erelt, P. Kahe võimu hääletoru. *Eesti Ekspress*, 2 May 2002.

The newspaper *Kodumaa*

It is not possible to identify Roolaht's writings in *Kodumaa*, because he published them under pseudonyms. It is nevertheless worth considering what the newspaper *Kodumaa* was when it began publication. The newspaper *Kodumaale Tagasipöördumise Eest* (*In the Name of Returning to the Homeland*) was officially published in Berlin from 1955 to 1958 and can be considered the indirect predecessor of *Kodumaa*. At the end of 1955, the ECP CC Bureau decided to make the editor of the newspaper *Rahva Hääl* (*People's Voice*) responsible for publishing the newspaper's Estonian-language newspaper for the diaspora, as the KGB had proposed. The newspaper's correspondents were chosen "from among the KGB's existing network of agents who had lived abroad in the past, selecting the kinds of agents who are capable of completing our assignments due to the nature of their work." KGB operative agents also used the occupation of newspaper correspondent as a cover.[18]

The ESSR KGB presented proposals for increasing the effectiveness of its work among Estonian expatriates, primarily in Sweden, to the ECP CC in September 1957. Among other things, the following was prescribed:

> "[...] 2. Organize the publication of a special newspaper with content appropriate for Estonians living abroad on the basis of the illustrated magazine *Pilt ja Sõna* (*Picture and Word*) that is issued in the Estonian SSR, and send it to Estonian emigrants. [...]

> "6. Organize the publication of the weekly newspaper *Estonia* in Estonian as the voice of the VOKS Estonian affiliate.[19] An editorial staff consisting of three persons is to be created for this purpose. This newspaper is to be distributed through free sale and subscriptions in the Estonian SSR as well as abroad. [...]

> "8. Practice the more active use of Soviet Estonia's periodicals and radio in order to expose the activities of reactionary emigrants against the people and disprove the slanderous fabrications that are being spread concerning conditions in contemporary Estonia.

> "The achievements of isolated emigrants in the field of folk literature, music, and art that deserve positive appraisal should also be noted in the pages of the press. [...]"[20]

---

[18] *Aruanne Eesti NSV MN juures asuva RJK 2. osakonna agentuur- ja operatiivtöö kohta 1956. aastal.* Tallinn: Rahvusarhiiv, 2000, 20, 59–60.

[19] The Estonian Society for Advancing Friendship and Cultural Ties Abroad.

[20] *Aruanne Eesti NSV MN juures asuva RJK 2. osakonna agentuur- ja operatiivtöö kohta 1957. aastal.* Tallinn: Rahvusarhiiv, 2002, 79–81.

The ECP CC formally approved the proposals and forwarded them to the Central Committee of the Communist Party of the Soviet Union (hereinafter referred to as the CPSU CC) for approval and coordination.[21] The proposals were implemented with certain changes. This was so only formally, because it could not have been a local initiative. In addition to the Estonian-language newspaper *Kodumaa*, the publication of similar newspapers began at the same time in the languages of other nationalities living in the western part of the Soviet Union: *Dzimtenes Balss* in Latvian, *Tevynes Balsas* in Lithuanian, *Radzima* in Byelorussian, *Haireniki Dzain* in Armenian, *Visti z Ukrainy* in Ukrainian, and in the 1960s, *Samšoblo* in Georgian.[22]

The ESSR KGB wrote the following in its yearly report to Moscow concerning 1958: "[…] The Fourth Department has also done work during the accounting period aimed at exerting a positive influence on the attitudes of rank-and-file emigrants and compromising leading Estonian emigrants. Thus publication of the Estonian-language weekly *Kodumaa* began in November of this year, as proposed by the Estonian KGB. Its circulation is 6,000 copies, and its objective is to disseminate truthful information concerning Soviet Estonia by describing the republic's economic and cultural development.

"Three thousand copies of this newspaper are distributed in the republic. The Estonian KGB, the newspaper's editorial office, and the Estonian Society for Maintaining Cultural Ties Abroad sends the other half of its circulation to known addresses of Estonian emigrants.

"The newspaper *Kodumaa* has aroused great interest among emigrants, as indicated by letters from emigrants and their relatives living in Estonia. For instance, someone named M. Sennel from West Germany writes to his relative in Tallinn that the newspaper *Kodumaa* that he received is very interesting and that he found out from the newspaper about radio broadcasts meant for emigrants. He heard voices speaking from his homeland for the first time.

"Someone named A. Anto from Switzerland writes to the Estonian Society for Maintaining Cultural Ties Abroad that he succeeded in getting hold of an issue of the newspaper *Kodumaa* by chance and now he would like to know if he can subscribe to that paper."[23]

---

[21] Ibid., 81.

[22] Imants Lešinskis. Kalpības gadi [Years of Servitude]. His memoirs were published in installments in the United States in the Latvian expatriate publication *Laiks* in 1979–1980. The complete text is available on the Internet: www.latvietislatvija.com/kalpibas_gadi-1.pdf *(14 November 2011). Imants Lešinskis was a Latvian SSR KGB officer responsible for propaganda who defected to the West.*

[23] *Aruanne Eesti NSV Ministrite Nõukogu juures asuva Riikliku Julgeoleku Komitee 4. Osakonna agentuur- ja operatiivtöö tulemuste kohta 1958. aastal. Tallinn: Rahvusarhiiv, 2005, 189–190.*

It is rightly mentioned concerning the report that "KGB personnel did not have any more such examples of 'great interest' among emigrants."[24] Nevertheless, the feedback obtained through the monitoring of correspondence was a convenient way for the KGB to correct the newspaper's content. Since researchers currently do not have access to Estonian SSR KGB reports submitted to Moscow after 1958 (they are currently kept in the Russian Federation), the use of this kind of method can only be surmised.

The newspaper's header included an interesting combination of symbols. The sea waves from the Estonian SSR's flag were used under Tallinn's skyline. *Kodumaa* was the only newspaper published in Estonia during the era of occupation that did not have the words, "Proletarians of all countries, unite!" on its masthead. Instead, it used the phrase, "Stand fast, you stalwart descendents of Kalev,[25] and may our homeland stand like a mighty rock!" (the first line of the Estonian SSR's anthem). It is noteworthy that the newspaper was often published in two colors, and in addition to the usual black printing ink, red, green, or blue printer's ink was used. The use of blue ink and black ink on white newsprint produced a color combination with recognizable Estonian national blue-black-white overtones.[26] The censors would not have allowed anything of the kind in Estonia's local papers before the late 1980s.

Kodumaa's primary theme was life in the Estonian SSR, more precisely how good life there was. Charts with rising lines and pictures of new industrial enterprises or of tractors in the fields with smiling workers or farmers were used in abundance to illustrate this good life. Naturally, such charts frequently had no connection with reality. At the same time, life did become somewhat better in the 1960s after the postwar trough. In the charts, comparisons with 1939 or 1940 were generally avoided. Stories concerning history did not appear in *Kodumaa* during its first years.

Pictures of old Tallinn, scenes of Estonia's nature, folk costumes, and other such scenes meant to put Estonians in a sentimental mood if they were far from home for a long time were prominent in the pictorial material used. This, of course, did not have much to do with Soviet reality, yet sometimes it could almost approximate the ideal propagated in the 1930s. For instance, a song festival advertisement depicting a young man and two young women in

---

[24] Enno Tammer, *Nõukogude piir ja lukus elu: meie mälestused.* Tallinn: Tammerraamat, 2008, 199.

[25] Kalev is a mythological hero from the Estonian national epic *Kalevipoeg* (Kalev's Son).

[26] Blue, black, and white are the colors of the Estonian national flag, which was banned during the Soviet occupation.

Estonian folk costumes standing on the seashore covered the entire front page in blue-and-black-on-white print of the 13 July 1963 issue of *Kodumaa*.

In addition to the positive aspects of the Estonian SSR, the Soviet Union and its achievements, progressiveness, and love of peace were all similarly promoted extensively. To a lesser extent, the paper strove to point out how the same kinds of attributes were missing in the West and in the prewar Republic of Estonia. An important theme in the paper's foreign news was the aggressiveness of NATO and especially of the United States and West Germany, as well as the machinations of their intelligence services. Great emphasis was placed on the Soviet Union's achievements in space technology and correspondingly on the U.S. failures in the same field. The paper never missed the chance to depict the entire American space program as the work of Wernher von Braun – that is to say, a Nazi – and American rockets as the descendents of the infamous German V-2 rockets.[27]

Many events organized by VEKSA were reported, such as trips by cultural figures to and from the Estonian SSR, as well as song festivals, elections, and speeches by leaders of the CPSU.

The first major treatment of a historical topic was an entire issue dedicated to the January 1962 trial in Tartu of Juhan Jüriste, Karl Linnas, and Ervin Viks.[28] A book in Estonian based on material from this trial was published for domestic use,[29] along with an English translation for distribution abroad.[30] Later, other "former Nazis" were often also severely criticized in *Kodumaa's* columns for both real and fabricated crimes. Historical themes were also taken up in the newspaper's supplement *Facts and Commentary*. This was published irregularly as a brochure.

The back page of the paper carried two regular columns. "Letters from the Folks at Home" contained letters from people living in Estonia who were

---

[27] This is more or less true. See, for instance, Weyer, J. *Wernher von Braun*. Tallinn: Olion, 2002.

[28] The accused were found guilty of crimes committed during World War II. A later investigation of the trial has shown that the charges most likely at least partially corresponded to the truth. At the same time, the event was largely oriented to propaganda, where even laws that applied in the Soviet Union were not observed. See Maripuu, M. Sõjakurjategijate protsessid ENSV Ülemkohtus – kohtupidamine või etendus (War Crimes Trials in the ESSR Supreme Court – Court Procedure or Performance). Supreme Court website: http://www.riigikohus. ee/vfs/742/ (14 November 2011).

[29] Lemmik, K. and Martinson, E. *12000: Tartus 16.–20. jaanuaril 1962 massimõrvarite Juhan Jüriste, Karl Linnase ja Ervin Viksi üle peetud kohtuprotsessi materjale.* Tallinn: Eesti Riiklik Kirjastus, 1962.

[30] Lemmik, K., and Martinson, E. *12,000: Materials from the Trial of the Mass Murderers Juhan Jüriste, Karl Linnas and Ervin Viks, held at Tartu on January 16–20, 1962.* Tallinn: Estonian State Publishing House, 1963.

seeking contact with relatives who had fled to the West in the tumult of war. It is likely that some of these letters were launched sent in the interests of the KGB. The column "Radio" contained radio frequencies and times of Soviet radio broadcasts intended for expatriate Estonians.

There were many different names among the authors of *Kodumaa's* articles, most of them pseudonyms. One could even get the impression that the paper had no editorial staff at all and that the paper's content consisted of the contributions of many individuals, although that was not the case. Many of the articles were written under pseudonyms, but the bylines of several people well-knownin the Estonian SSR could also be found in the paper. For instance, KGB officer Randar Hiir wrote for the paper under his own name, though he did not reveal what his job was.[31]

Roolaht's books on history

The largest project that Andrus Roolaht accomplished was volumes XI through XV of the compendium of articles *Eesti riik ja rahvas II maailmasõjas* (The State and People of Estonia in World War II), published in 1964–1972.[32] Roolaht used the help of others to some extent in the completion

---

[31] Hiir, R. Abiks võõrsil elavatele eestlastele (Help for Estonians Living Abroad). *Kodumaa*, 31 January 1961.

[32] The author is not indicated in the books, and direct documentary evidence concerning Roolaht's authorship has not been found. There is, however, a certain amount of more indirect evidence. Head of the University of Tallinn Center of Expatriate Estonian Literature Anne Valmas has named Roolaht as the author of volumes XI–XV of *Eesti riik ja rahvas II maailmasõjas* (Anne Valmas, the Collection of Expatriate Estonian Literature and Databases at the University of Tallinn Academic Library, presentation at the 2006 International Conference of Expatriate Baltic Archives. Museum of Estonian Literature website.<http://www.kirmus.ee/baltic_archives_abroad_2006/kogumik/Valmas.htm>[12 January 2009]). His authorship was asserted in the press during Roolaht's lifetime as well (Erelt, P. Kahe võimu hääletoru. *Eesti Ekspress*, 2 May 2002), and he did not refute it. The text published in volumes XI–XV is later repeated in Andrus Roolaht's book written under the pseudonym Rein Kordes. A1967 letter about Roolaht states: "He has written a series of articles and published collected works that tell of the anti-Soviet activity of leading emigrants and have contributed to dissention in emigrant organizations." (Character assessment-recommendation, A. Mihhailov, H. Toomsalu, E. Moorman, 24 July 1967, ERAF.136SM.1.2934, 18). No other collected works corresponding to this description are known to have been published by that time besides volumes XI and XII of *Eesti riik ja rahvas II maailmasõjas*; Roolaht has mentioned volumes XI–XV as "works of counter-propaganda completed in the ESSR Academy of Sciences Academic Library" in the overview he provided of the work of his sector (Roolaht ECP CC to the VSO, 5 April 1980, TLÜ TR VEKK). Even this is not firm proof, because the sector did not actually exist at the time that the books were published.

of these volumes.[33] This was the Soviet response to the compendium that was published in Stockholm in 1954–1962 and dealt chronologically with Estonian history from the 1930s until the second Soviet occupation.

The work was aimed at expatriate Estonians, and the selection of themes followed from this. Unlike domestic historical literature, there was no point in glorifying the ECP's role or in writing about the persecution of the Bolsheviks in the Republic of Estonia. The official Soviet version of the events of 1940 obviously would not have been acceptable either for people who had lived through those events themselves. Since the German occupation had been milder for Estonians than the Soviet occupation of 1940–1941, the glorification of the Red Army for "liberating Estonia from fascist invaders" in 1944 would also not have paid off.

From the analysis of these books, it appears that Soviet propaganda attempted not to create new conflicts among the more active expatriates but instead to use conflicts that already existed. Memoirs and exile periodicals provided abundant material for learning about these conflicts. Data received from the KGB's network of agents might also have been used. Four of the most important categories should be pointed out from among the conflicts that were used in books:

First, the Estonian prewar Ministry of Foreign Affairs vs. the General Staff, in other words which of them was guilty (or more guilty) of losing Estonia's independence in 1939–1940. It is not quite clear whether there was such a conflict in the late 1930s, and if so, how sharp it actually was. Former employees of the Ministry of Foreign Affairs claimed in the 1950s that these conflicts existed and naturally, former officers reacted to this.

Second, democracy vs. the "Era of Silence"[34] (in other words, the supporters of Jaan Tõnisson from the political left and the members of the right-wing War of Independence veterans movement vs. the supporters of Konstantin Päts). These political conflicts existed in Estonian society since the 1920s, and the 1934 coup d'état served only to exacerbate them. Criticism that

---

[33] It appears from Roolaht's investigation file in the archive's special section that he has indeed viewed materials used in many, but not all, of the subsequent volumes of *Eesti riik ja rahvas II maailmasõjas*. For instance, there is no evidence that he has perused materials from archive 957 (Ministry of Foreign Affairs), but materials in that archive have been used. The possibility that the file does not reflect his entire activity cannot be ruled out. Roolaht has indicated the theme of his research study as writing volume XII of *Eesti riik ja rahvas II maailmasõjas* but not the remaining volumes: Riigiarhiiv (National Archives) ERA.R-18.5.204.

[34] The "Era of Silence" is a name widely used in historiography for the period 1934–1938/40 in Estonian history. In that period parliamentary democracy was suppressed, and the press was censored.

could not be published in silent-era Estonia due to censorship could be freely published after the war in exile.

Third, supporters of the Western Allies vs. supporters of Germany during World War II (in other words: Anglophiles vs. collaborators). This theme was used particularly often in published English-language résumés beginning with volume XII of *Eesti riik ja rahvas...*.

Fourth, conflicts between individuals. These could readily be found, and the antagonists frequently did not keep it between themselves. It was relatively easy to obtain information concerning conflicts from the expatriate press, and Soviet propaganda only had to try to fan the flames from time to time.

The recommendation to exploit conflicts between expatriate Estonians was also prescribed in KGB theory. The following was written in the co-unterintelligence handbook: "The use of conflicts in the anti-Soviet camp of Estonian emigrants, which are inherent to all anti-Soviet emigrant organizations, is of significant importance to KGB organs and their work in breaking down and compromising expatriate Estonian nationalist organizations."[35]

Another popular theme was corruption in the prewar Republic of Estonia. This could, and apparently did, cause disgust and perhaps also jealousy in many expatriate Estonians. Some individuals might withdraw from active political work (or, at least, so the KGB hoped) out of fear that they would be the next target of the Soviet propaganda machine.

In terms of individuals, the general rule was that the more politically active an expatriate was, the greater the likelihood that he would be attacked in KGB publications. A running theme was naturally the fascist sympathies of some expatriates before and during World War II and the fascist sympathies of the Republic of Estonia as a whole. Expatriate Estonian historical literature is, among other things, accused of "glorifying members of the SS."[36]

The publications were based on the thesis that there was an emigrant "upper crust" with a negative attitude towards the Soviet Union and ordinary expatriates who were neutral towards the Soviet Union. KGB reports received from abroad fed this notion,[37] and the leadership of the Estonian SSR probably also believed it. Publications aimed at expatriate Estonians

---

[35] Entry: *Эстонские зарубежные националистические организации.* Контрразведыва-тельный словарь. Москва: Вышая краснознаменная школа Комитета Государственной Безопасности при Совете Министров СССР им. Ф. Э. Дзержинского, 1972, p. 368;

[36] *Eesti riik ja rahvas II maailmasõjas, XI.* Tallinn: Kodumaa, 1964, 6.

[37] See, for example, the detailed overview compiled in 1962 by Vsevolod Naidyonkov: Esto-nian emigrants in Sweden: ERAF.1.254.23, 62–125. (Naidyonkov was an undercover KGB officer at one time attached to the Soviet Embassy in Stockholm.)

attempted to discredit the "upper crust" and thus win ordinary expatriates over to the Soviet camp. The foreword of volume XI states that "the articles in this collected work have been written only due to the stale rule by clique prevailing in the backyards of the emigrant upper crust, meaning plotting, hating one another, jealousy, undermining, and so on."[38] Indeed, this is a distorted reflection of expatriate Estonian historical literature, and there are very few influences from the Estonian SSR historiography of that time.

There are also examples of fabrications in Roolaht's works. The story concerning Leo Talgre, the intelligence organizer involved in resistance, that appeared in volume XV is the one that has been most thoroughly researched. This story appeared in 1965 under the pseudonym K. Saarse as a *Kodumaa* supplement[39] and was published again in 1976 under the name Rein Kordes[40] (see also the memoirs of Maarja Talgre, below). The circumstances of Leo Talgre's death in these publications are completely false. He was killed in an exchange of fire with Soviet security agents in Tallinn on 17 December 1944. According to Roolaht, however, his corpse was found in the woods in January 1945. The remainder of the text is primarily based on Leo Talgre's diary. However, some entries that Roolaht purports to quote from Talgre's diary have in fact been fabricated, creating a negative picture not only of Talgre himself but also of people who came into contact with him (such as the Estonian ambassador in Finland, Aleksander Warma, after the war one of the leading persons among the Estonian emigres).

The design of *Eesti riik ja rahvas...* XI–XV copied the book of the same name designed by Otto Paju and published in Sweden in 1954–1962. Only the color combination was altered. The foreword of volume XI, published in Soviet Estonia, notes concerning volumes I–X that the "typographical workmanship is a credit to the printing plant." The same can also be said about volumes XI–XV: these books were printed on better quality paper than most publications of the Estonian SSR. The result created quite an authentic impression; it was, justifiably, probably hoped that volumes XI–XV would find their place on the bookshelf beside volumes I–X. Unlike volumes I–X, the continuation volumes do not include a single reference to the author of the text. It was only stated that the current book was a publication of the newspaper *Kodumaa* and that it was printed at the Kommunist Printing House. Later on, even that information was not mentioned in the book. Even

---

[38] *Eesti riik ja rahvas II maailmasõjas, XI*, 6.

[39] Saarse, K. Leo Talgre "tähelend" (Leo Talgre's "Meteoric Flight"). *Faktid ja kommentaarid, Kodumaa* supplement, 1965.

[40] Kordes, Rein. *Mineviku teed ja rajad*. Tallinn: Perioodika, 1976, 290–299.

information concerning print run, submission for typesetting, and other such information that was compulsory in books published in the USSR is missing.[41] Its index of names and brief summary in English also added to its seemingly academic appearance.

Like the continuation volumes of *Eesti riik ja rahvas II maailmasõjas*, *Eesti emigrantide saatusaastad* (*The Fateful Years of Estonian Emigrants, 1974–80*)[42] is a Soviet reaction to the collected work *Eesti saatusaastad* (*Estonia's Fateful Years, 1963–72*) that appeared abroad.[43] Unlike Roolaht's earlier books, now the author is indicated – Rein Kordes – in addition to all the publishing information required in the USSR (printed in Russian on the last page of the book, including the book's print run and price – twenty-five kopeks). The format and external appearance of the book published in Sweden is no longer copied, not to mention the quality of the paper. The English summary has been omitted, but the index of names has been preserved.

Roolaht has again used a "collage technique" (his own expression), consisting mainly of retelling what has appeared in the expatriate press. Excerpts from earlier books are interspersed. Brief notations with neutral or even outright positive content, usually about cultural figures and found in obituaries, are a novelty. For instance, the results of studies that indicate that Estonian culture and the Estonian language are dying out are set out in a neutral tone. These are apparently added in part to make the books more readable. The relatively large number of obituaries creates a rather morose impression when reading the books, and it was evidently intended to have that kind of effect on expatriates, to entrench the feeling of the inevitability of the dying out of the expatriate Estonian community.

Mineviku teed ja rajad (*Roads and Paths of the Past*) appeared in 1976[44] and is a compilation of Roolaht's earlier books. The ESTO festival could have been the reason for its publication. Expatriates celebrated the worldwide ESTO festival beginning in 1972 and every four years thereafter. Then, as well as in 1976 and 1980, a new publication by Andrus Roolaht appeared prior to the event. It is possible that the second part of *Eesti emigrantide saatusaastad* was not ready for printing by the time of the 1976 ESTO festival in Baltimore

---

[41] *Mittesalajaste väljaannete trükkimise ühtsed eeskirjad* (Unified regulations for printing non-secret publications). Tallinn: Main Administration for Protecting State Secrets in Printed Matter under the USSR Council of Ministers, 1967, § 14.

[42] Kordes, R. *Eesti emigrantide saatusaastad, I–III.* Tallinn: Perioodika, 1974, 1978, 1980.

[43] *Eesti saatusaastad, I–VI.* Stockholm: EMP, 1963–1972.

[44] Kordes, *Mineviku teed ja rajad.*

but that the authorities wanted to issue something to counterbalance that event and so *Mineviku teed ja rajad* was used to fill that gap.

In reference to the last four books, historian Indrek Jürjo has quite pointedly written: "Compromising affairs plucked from the expatriate Estonian press and memoirs mingle in these lampoons with direct fabrications and slander in a manner characteristic of the KGB's exposé literature and with vague references to some sort of archival documents or manuscripts that Roolaht has, in some mysterious way, gotten a hold of."[45] Roolaht himself was of a different opinion. In 2002, the journalist Pekka Erelt asked him: "After the war, you wrote sharply critical propaganda books for expatriate Estonians. Do you regret that now or not?" There is no regret in Roolaht's reply: "Everything in those books is true. Everything is based on archival documents or personal memory. Edit out only the derogatory expressions of those times, and what you are left with is completely objective historical material."[46] As what is written about Leo Talgre demonstrates, he relied here and there not only on memory and archival sources but also simply on fantasy. However, it remains uncertain whether Roolaht himself generated the ideas or whether the KGB did it.

Roolaht's last publication that appeared under the name of Kordes was an "annotation" to a book by August Ots[47] and bore the title *See, millest avalikult ei räägita* (*What Is Not Mentioned in Public*).[48] Ots was a vehement opponent of Päts and Laidoner, and his book was sharply critical as well. Apparently unwittingly, it was already partially influenced by what had been published in the Estonian SSR.[49] Roolaht briefly summarized the text and picked out the juicier quotations from it. He did not distort August Ots's words, yet the brochure had a significantly larger circulation than the annotated book did.

Andrus Roolaht's works of propaganda have not left a visible trace in historiography. Since they are so clearly part of the political propaganda published in the tense times of the Cold War, later historians have not referenced them as sources of truth, so to speak. The works are in Estonian,

---

[45] Jürjo, *Pagulus ja Nõukogude Eesti*, 229.

[46] Erelt, "Kahe võimu hääletoru."

[47] Ots, August, *Miks kaotasime iseseisvuse: Eestluse probleeme eksiilis* (Why We Lost Our Independence: Estonian Problems in Exile). Stockholm: Välis-Eesti & EMP, 1981.

[48] Kordes, Rein, *See, millest avalikult ei räägita: annotatsioon A. Otsa uuele raamatule*. Tallinn: Perioodika, 1981.

[49] Ots has used some claims on German-Estonian intelligence cooperation before World War II. Although he got the information from a book published in West Germany, it originated from the Estonian SSR KGB. For more details on the case, see: Juurvee, Ivo. KGB, Stasi ja Eesti luureajalugu. *Tuna* 2 (2008), 32–53.

and thus historians from other countries, who may perhaps have erred in source criticism due to unfamiliarity with the background of those works, have also not been able to use them.

Roolaht's books and articles contributed somewhat to creating tension between individuals in the expatriate Estonian community. Yet they definitely made the atmosphere there unpleasant and caused mental suffering for those close to the persons lied about in Roolaht's works, as we can see from Maarja Talgre's description of her personal experiences below.

Annex: My memories
of Soviet propaganda in Sweden[1]

Maarja Talgre

My beginning was in Estonia, but I was born in Sweden on 27 February 1945, when my mother Melanie was in a refugee camp together with my aunt, grandfather, and grandmother. My father, Leo Talgre, was a successful and energetic figure in Estonia's resistance movement.

When Hitler started losing the war and retreated from Estonia in the autumn of 1944, it was clear that Stalin would be back soon. On 20 September 1944, Leo packed my mother's little suitcase with mother's photographs and his own suit, binoculars, a windbreaker, and money in several different currencies. He sent my mother with me in her tummy, together with her parents and sister, out of Estonia on a Finnish speedboat. Father hoped to follow after us when his duties as a freedom fighter were done. My family made it to Sweden through a terrible storm and difficulties. We struggled in our new country, found ourselves a place to live, and started waiting for my father. We waited and waited, but neither information nor the person we were waiting for could get through Stalin's Iron Curtain.

I waited for my father all my childhood. I went to meet him on the highway. I dreamed about him. I very much longed for him. But nothing helped. Father did not come. My father Leo's absence was like a huge black hole inside me. I had seen him in photographs, and I had been told that he was forced to stay in Estonia and fight against Stalin.

I was terribly afraid of Stalin as a little child. At night I listened to the freight trains passing through my home town, Partille. Sometimes some train braked or started going more slowly. Then I hid my head under the blanket and held my breath. So that Stalin wouldn't find me. I had heard my family talk about how Stalin put Estonian children, women, and men in

---

[1]   The memoirs of Swedish Estonian Maarja Talgre are added as the second viewpoint to Ivo Juurvee's research to illustrate the reality of the Soviet propaganda measures among the Estonian diaspora in Sweden.

cattle cars and took them to Siberia. I quivered with fear until I crept into my grandmother and grandfather's bed. Grandfather snored, and I hoped that if Stalin heard my grandfather snoring, then he wouldn't have the courage to come in through our door. At home, I had been told that Hitler was the same kind of criminal as Stalin. Luckily, Hitler was dead even before I was born, and when Stalin died in 1953, I literally danced with relief. All the same, my grandfather said that there were still plenty of dangerous men like Malenkov and Molotov still alive in Moscow.

But we continued to fear the NKVD, which by then may already have been the KGB. The Soviets kept an eye on us even though we lived in Sweden. The KGB tortured us with its newspaper *Kodumaa*. I pricked up my ears to listen to the talk between refugees when they met at parties. The birthday coffee cake might be plentiful and the coffee might taste very good – there could be plenty of laughter and song. But fear was already long since in the coffee-cake dough, in people's hearts and voices when they suddenly quietly asked each other.

> – Was it in your mailbox, too?
> – No, luckily not yet.
> – My neighbor received *Kodumaa* yesterday. So the security organs already have his address.

Each family that received the newspaper *Kodumaa* in their home mailbox knew it already from its foreign stench. The newspaper *Kodumaa* stank. It didn't smell. The stench was sharp and different from Swedish newspapers. The stench reminded us of the danger and uncertainty of our situation. That same uncertainty that convinced many people to leave Sweden: to America, Canada, Australia, and Argentina. As far as possible from Soviet rule.

Finally, when my grandfather Rudolf had long since passed away and I was in university, a long article about my father appeared in the *Kodumaa* supplement. The title of the supplement was *Facts and Commentary*. The year was 1965. Its price was two kopeks. The article's title was "Leo Talgre's Meteoric Flight," and it was written by someone named K. Saarse. It was discussed a great deal at home, but when I asked to read it, my mother replied: "You know, you'd be better off not to read it. The story is terrible and false propaganda. It'll only hurt you." And when I saw my mother's facial expression, I gave up the idea of reading it. My mother's face was white and somehow strained. As if she were in great physical pain. Mother put that issue of *Kodumaa* in a plastic bag and hid it under shoes and socks in the closet.

But even though "Leo Talgre's Meteoric Flight" was buried at the bottom of the closet, it grated against my soul. My mother gave my father's clothes an airing every spring. We worried for a long time, feeling something between hope and mourning. Who was that person who tried to smear my father's honor and honesty?

It was only many years later, in 1988, that I dared to read what K. Saarse had written. By then I had become an employee of Swedish Radio's Culture Department. I was also a Swedish writer and lecturer. And most importantly, I had my own family. My daughter Lina started asking who her grandfather was and what had become of him. The time had come to take the KGB's poisonous snake out of Mother's closet. I approached the snake like a journalist and a writer. I had to put on my professional suit because Leo's daughter was too soft. His daughter was still that child who waited every evening for her father when other fathers came home from the city by train carrying their suitcases from the office.

It took me three weeks to manage to read "Leo Talgre's Meteoric Flight" through to the end. I came down with a fever, I was overcome with nausea, and even though I knew that the story was KGB propaganda, every line still had an effect. Because when you see something in print, it creates some kind of deceptive documentary effect. The article begins:

> "The frozen corpse of a young man was found in a Harju County forest area in January 1945. It appeared from the papers found in his pockets that it was the mortal remains of the fascist intelligence agent Leo Talgre. [...] There were other papers in the pockets of the corpse aside from identification documents. These papers verified that Leo Talgre (whose former name was Bibikov) was one of the leaders of the fascist counterintelligence espionage group Abwehrkommando 166. His career began in the spring of 1941. Four years later he was lying in a snow bank as food for foxes."

My father, Leo Talgre, attended Tallinn Technical University and was a talented athlete when Stalin launched his first occupation in 1940. Leo succeeded in escaping on skis over the ice to Finland in 1941. He did not want to end up in the Red Army. The Finns offered him training in counter-intelligence, and Leo decided to dedicate himself to liberating Estonia. He participated in both the Erna and Haukka groups. Later he worked in Cellarius's counterintelligence bureau. That was his secret work. In reality, he worked in the Estonian resistance movement. His last assignment was to save Estonia's provisional government by helping it get to Sweden when Stalin was returning. The boat, however, was late and went to the wrong place. The government, Leo, the freedom fighters, and the Estonian people were caught in the palm of Stalin's hand.

But back to the *Kodumaa* supplement, where KGB servant K. Saarse, alias Andrus Roolaht, alias Otto Roser and also under the pseudonym Rein Kordes, serves up this entire sad story of Estonia in World War II in his own way in order to affirm the Soviet version of history and to smear Estonian patriots. Roolaht uses something that he refers to as "Leo Talgre's diary," of which there is even a photograph with the caption "Leo Talgre's diary is full of facts."

Roolaht/K. Saarse quotes certain selected parts and claims, "Leo Talgre very meticulously kept a diary." What is deceptive is that some excerpts seem to be authentic, because my father Leo kept a diary almost every day from 1938 until his death.

> Roolaht's "example": 17 April 1943:
> "Arrived in Tartu 11:50. [...] I change my clothes at Mrs. Milk's place…Liivika's anniversary in the evening. Conversation in the tower at the anniversary. Moods." My father was a member of the Liivika university students' society, and Mrs. Milk was also in the resistance movement and a good friend of Leo together with her husband. Yet in the same article, Roolaht gives free rein to his fantasy. For me the most loathsome fabrication is this: "Before taking his new position, Leo Talgre nevertheless had to go through several crash courses related to his occupation. The final touches were put on the new spy in Leningrad oblast, where he served as acting warden of a concentration camp for a few months and personally participated in the mass destruction of prisoners of war and civilians. This executioner's work was an inseparable component of Hitlerite teachings. That joined Leo Talgre to fascism once and for all and cut off all ways back for him [...] At the beginning of his career, Leo Talgre firmly believed that Hitler's plans for conquest were realistic and hoped that he too would soon be part of the ranks of the fascist elite."

Some other excerpts from Roolaht's KGB article were so absurd that they seemed comical to me even in 1988, when I read it for the first time: "Leo Talgre's diary shows that its author was a typical idle intellectual of the kind that was widespread at that time who didn't really know how to do anything. His strongest asset was his skill in making useful acquaintances and in knowing how to behave politely in 'polite society.' In all probability, he absolutely lacked any intellectual interests whatsoever. Leo Talgre dedicated all his free time to boozing and women. The sexual fantasy of this young man, who had just recently grown out of puberty, knew no bounds. Every encounter, which usually took place when intoxicated by alcohol, was the discovery of a 'new world' – frequently with several partners in one night."

At this point, I will discontinue quoting K. Saarse's alias Andrus Roolaht's long article, which has so greatly injured my family and me. When I went to Estonia in 1988 to question people about my father and his activities, I brought a copy of the *Kodumaa* article with me. Everyone read it with keen interest. And for their own part, they explained how the resistance movement operated and what kind of person my father was. I went to *Kodumaa's* editorial office to look for the author. I visited Felix Kauba to investigate the death of my father, since Kauba had been there when he died. Kauba was the head of the Academy of Sciences Library and was connected to the KGB. All forbidden books published in the West were under his supervision. Felix Kauba confirmed that the corpse partially eaten by foxes was a falsification: "I can assure you of that, since your father died in my arms." Kauba described my father's death. My father was shot by an NKVD soldier in a house where Kauba himself lived temporarily. I have written about all that in my book *Leo ett estnisk töde* (*Leo – Resistance till Death*, translated by Anu Saluäär).

What interested me, of course, was whether the *Kodumaa* author really had read my father's diaries. Kauba telephoned Roolaht in my presence. Kauba was Roolaht's former boss at the ESSR Academy of Sciences Library. Roolaht told Kauba that he had indeed read them, since journalists were able to gain access to the KGB archives during a somewhat more liberal period in the 1960s.

When Estonia became free again, I went to the KGB archives to look for my father's diaries. But they weren't there. The historian Mart Laar had been there as a historian immediately before Estonia regained its independence but had not found the diaries. Mart Laar wrote a very interesting epilogue for my book.

Over the years, I went looking for Andrus Roolaht several times. Shortly before his death, I got hold of him by telephone. As soon as the old man heard my name, he said: "Why did you write spitefully about me in your book?"

Me: "Why did you write so horridly about my father in the *Kodumaa* supplement?"

Roolaht: "That's how people had to write back then. It was part and parcel of writing."

Me: "I'd like to know if you really have read my father's diaries in the KGB archives."

Roolaht: "Yes, I have."

Did Andrus Roolaht lie to me until his death? I am not certain about that. The whole story "Leo Talgre's Meteoric Flight" is, of course, a falsification and loathsome propaganda to me. What makes it even more dreadful is that Roolaht is a skilled KGB propagandist. It looks like he has some genuine documents at his disposal, but he uses them like raisins in his propaganda cake. He distorts facts and fantasizes in between.

A couple of years ago, I found most of my father's diaries. They had been hidden in Canada, and the good person who found them had read my book. I now have possession of my father's diaries. I read them and I know quite precisely where he was, what he did, and what he was thinking. But the last months prior to Leo's death on 17 December 1944 are missing. Roolaht writes that Leo's diaries, which he had read, end on 16 December 1944. If I sort out Roolaht's article, I find a couple of extracts that really appear to be authentic. They just might be those diaries that I am missing.

But where did they disappear to after Roolaht read them? Did they again end up in the hands of some malevolent power or person? That question makes my heart ache.

The Remains of Communist Identity in Slovenia. Transitional Justice in Slovenia: Potential, Pitfalls, and Future

Jernej Letnar Černič

Introduction

The shaping of communist identity and personality has left ineradicable scars in the landscape of the present-day Slovene democratic society. In the twentieth century the Republic of Slovenia (hereinafter Slovenia) was subjected to three forms of totalitarian system or regime: Italian fascism, Nazism, and communism. Slovenia is therefore the only EU member state that has been subjected to all three totalitarian regimes. All three forms of totalitarian regime in Slovenia had common and comparable characteristics. Jože Dežman, a Slovenian historian, notes that all three forms included "abuse of national sentiment to carry out racial and class revolutionary projects; cult of a great leader, who permits his fanatics to murder, steal, and lie; dictatorship of one party; militarization of society, police state – almighty secret political police; collectivism, subjection of the citizen to the totalitarian state; state terrorism with systematic abuses of basic human rights; aggressive assumption of power and struggle for territory."[1] It must be noted that all three forms of totalitarian regime in Slovenia attempted to monitor and regulate every aspect of public and private life by every means wherever feasible. Furthermore, it must be noted that fascism, Nazism, and communism in Slovenia differed in their duration. Whereas the Nazi occupation of Slovenia lasted from 1941 to 1945, the fascist totalitarian system governed Slovenia from 1919 to 1943. The longest-lasting totalitarian regime in Slovenia was the totalitarian communist regime, which officially terrorized Slovenia from the end of World War II in 1945 to the first democratic

---

[1] Dežman, J. Communist Repression and Transitional Justice in Slovenia. In Jambrek, P. (ed.). *Crimes Committed by Totalitarian Regimes: Slovenian Presidency of the Council of the European Union, Bruxelles*. Ljubljana, 2008, 197.

elections in April 1990, when the opposition political parties united in the DEMOS movement. However, the communist totalitarian regime began much earlier, during World War II, when the Communist Party monopolized the resistance movement.

Section II of the present work briefly outlines the factual background of the communist crimes committed in Slovenia. This is followed by a discussion and analysis of transitional justice measures in Slovenia in Section III. Section IV discusses symbols of the totalitarian or repressive past, trying to draw lessons concerning the understanding of current ideological and political divisions in Slovenian public space. Finally, Section V examines reconciliation measures in Slovenia and lays the basis for the argument that there exists a strong legal and moral ground for prosecuting perpetrators of crimes against humanity. In this way, this article thereafter analyzes the consequences and influences of the shaping of communist identity in Slovenia, trying to draw out lessons concerning the understanding of current ideological divisions in Slovenia. Equipped with this knowledge, this article goes on to argue that consensus appears to be growing for meaningful and continued reform, which would attempt to remove the consequences and influences of the shaping of communist identity in Slovenia.

The communist totalitarian regime in Slovenia

The communist regime was the longest-lasting totalitarian regime administering and terrorizing the territory of Slovenia. The communist totalitarian regime officially governed Slovenia from the end of World War II until the first democratic elections in April 1990. However, the beginnings of the communist regime can be traced back to World War II, that is, the late 1930s. The communist system gradually assumed more control starting with the Nazi occupation of Slovenia in 1941, when it monopolized the resistance movement against the occupation and launched a communist-style revolution.[2] The communist totalitarian regime maintained its power through revolutionary violence, a culture of fear, crimes against humanity, against a civilian population, show judicial proceedings, nationalization and confiscation of property, labor and concentration camps, the elimination of political opponents, and the banning of any type of opposition. The

---

[2] Hančič, D., Podberšič, R., and Ivanc B. Slovenia: From Triple Totalitarian Occupation to Freedom and Independence. In Kühnhardt, L. (ed.). *The Reunification of Europe, Anti-Totalitarian Courage and Political Renewal*. European Parliament, EPP-ED Group, 2009, 372.

communist totalitarian period must be divided into two main periods. The first period is from the end of the war in 1945 until the first months of 1950, and the second period is from the beginning of the 1950s until the fall of the communist regime in 1990.

Božo Repe notes that "during the war, the Communist Party in Slovenia, which organized and operationally controlled the resistance against occupiers, began articulating revolutionary goals"[3] and "in March 1943, the Slovenian Communist Party persuaded a number of non-communist groups in the Slovenian Liberation Front to unify under communist leadership."[4] A part of the population organized and formed the "Village Guards" and later (after Italy's capitulation in September 1943) the Home Guard, which resisted the monopolization of the resistance movement by the Communist Party.[5] This resulted in a civil war between members of the Slovenian Liberation Front and members of the Village Guards and Home Guard,[6] particularly during the massacres of non-communist members of the Slovenian National Front in 1943. The political opponents of the Slovenian Communist Party were mostly Christian Democrats, who refused to join the National Liberation movement.

The Slovenian Liberation Front won the armed conflict with German and Italian forces and liberated Slovenia. In this way, the Slovenian Communist Party seized the opportunity to turn a national liberation movement against the Axis forces from a resistance struggle into a civil war, and it prohibited those who did not accept Communist Party leadership from fighting against the occupiers. In other words, the partisan movement led by the Slovenian Communist Party won the civil war. The most common communist totalitarian crimes during the period 1945–1951 included mass extrajudicial killings or crimes against humanity, the construction of concentration and labor camps, forced deprivations of liberty, the arranging of show and political trials, deportations abroad of inhabitants, and the suppression of religion and persecution of the church and clergy.

After World War II the Communist Party carried out a systematic and widespread campaign of extrajudicial mass killing against "national enemies," which were mostly comprised of unarmed civilians – men, women, and children. At the end of World War II, given the advance of Partisan guerrillas and after an unsuccessful attempt to establish their own parliament and

---

[3]   Repe, B. Slovenia during the Second World War. http://www.theslovenian.com/articles/
2008/repe1.pdf (last visited 10 November 2009).
[4]   Ibid.
[5]   Ibid.
[6]   Ibid.

government in May 1945, the political opponents of the Communist Party (the Slovenian National Army) fled to the British Occupation Zone in Carinthia and were placed in a camp at Vetrinj.[7] At the end of May 1945, the British troops handed over 30,000 men to Tito's communist forces.[8] Most of them were subsequently executed in forests and caves all across Slovenia. Only after the fall of the Iron Curtain and the totalitarian regimes did secret gravesites begin to be made public. As many as 130,000 persons are estimated to have been summarily executed on Slovenian territory in the months following the end of World War II on 9 May 1945.[9] An estimated 15,000 of those executed were of Slovenian nationality, while the others were Croats, Serbs, and Germans. They were mostly civilians, but they also included members of the Slovenian Home Guards and other political opponents of the resistance movement led by the Slovenian Communist Party. These crimes consisted mostly of systematic executions at hidden locations all across Slovenia, predominantly in unpopulated rural areas and in forests, and were carried out by members of the Slovenian section of the Yugoslav Secret Police.[10] They were part of retaliation after World War II but are also alleged to be part of a plan to eliminate part of Slovenia's civilian population.

Mitja Ferenc notes that "methodical record-keeping of secret mass graves only began in 2002, accompanied by a huge response in the media triggered

---

[7] See T. Giesser Pečar, p. 529.

[8] Ibid. See also Cogwill, A., Brimelow, T., and Booker, C. *The Repatriation from Austria in 1945: The Report of an Inquiry.* London: Sinclair-Stevenson Ltd., 1990; Mitchell, I. *The Cost of a Reputation: Aldington Versus Tolstoy; The Causes, Course and Consequences of the Notorious Libel Case,* Glasgow: Canongate Books Ltd, 1997; Nicolson, N. *Long Life: Memoirs.* New York: Putnam, 1998. See also Corsellus, J., and Ferrar, M. *Slovenia 1945: Memories of Death and Survival After World War II.* London and New York: I.B. Tauris & Co. Ltd., 2005.

[9] Pavel Jamnik's statement on the program *Polemika*, RTV Slovenia, 9 March 2009. The exact number of people executed is unknown. The estimates vary between 100,000 and 130,000. See also Jamnik, P. Post-World War Two Crimes on the Territory of Slovenia: Police Investigation and Proof regarding Criminal Offenses that Do Not Fall under the Statute of Limitations. *Crimes Committed by Totalitarian,* 207. See also Dežman, op. cit., 204; Vodopivec, P. *Od Pohlinove slovnice do samostojne države: slovenska zgodovina od konca 18. stoletja do konca 20. stoletja.* Modrijan, 2006. The author gives the number of 100,000 to 130,000 people killed on Slovenian territory. This opinion is shared by Slovenian historians Dr. Tone Ferenc and Jože Dežman. See also Starič, J.V. *Kako se čistila Jugoslavija?* Gordogan, 2004, 36–50. Furthermore, Ljubo Sirc notes that the total number of victims is "estimated to be between 150,000 and 200,000" (Sirc, L. Totalitarian Features of the Judiciary in Slovenia (1945–1990): Disregard for the Rule of Law. *Crimes Committed by Totalitarian,* 135.

[10] Pučnik, J. Mass Post-War Killings. In Jančar, D. (ed.). *The Dark Side of the Moon: A Short History of Totalitarianism in Slovenia 1945–1990.* Ljubljana: Muzej novejše zgodovine, 1998, 39–52.

by discovery of 431 victims from two shafts in Zgornja Bistrica in Štajerska."[11] The Ministry of Labor, Family, and Social Affairs of the Republic of Slovenia has catalogued 3,986 wartime mass graves in Slovenia from World War II.[12] This data does not include the secret mass graves. As noted above, the Commission for Settlement of Hidden Mass Graveyards of the Government of the Republic of Slovenia, particularly through the work of Ferenc, has so far catalogued almost 600 hidden mass gravesites found on the territory of Slovenia.[13] Ferenc divides the locations of posthumous remains into four groups: pits; mineshafts and shelters; anti-tank and previously excavated shafts; and karst abysses. In this way, Map 1 illustrates the secret mass gravesites that have thus far been found on the territory of Slovenia.

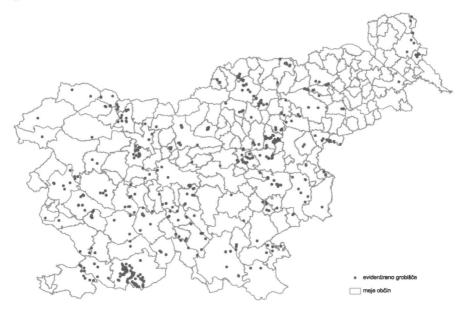

Figure 1: Identified secret mass graves on the territory of Slovenia
Source: Ferenc, M. Topografija evidentiranih grobišč. *Poročilo Komisije vlade Republike Slovenije za reševanje vprašanj prikritih grobišč: 2005–2008*. Ljubljana: Družina, 2008, 25.

---

[11] Ferenc, M. Secret World War Two Mass Graves in Slovenia. *Crimes Committed by Totalitarian*, 158.

[12] Ibid., 155.

[13] For a detailed historical account, see Ferenc, M. Topografija evidentiranih grobišč. *Poročilo Komisije vlade Republike Slovenije za reševanje vprašanj prikritih grobišč: 2005–2008*. Ljubljana: Družina, 2008; Griesser-Pecar, T. *Das zerrissene Volk. Slowenien 1941–1946*. Vienna: Böhlau, 2003. See also Šturm, L. *Brez milosti: ranjeni, invalidni in bolni povojni ujetniki na Slovenskem*. Ljubljana: Nova revija, 2000.

Ferenc notes that for most of those in secret mass graves and individual graves, as well as other victims, "it is not even known where they lie, and they never received a burial worthy of a human being." He continues that "crimes were exacerbated by forced silence and suppression of the right to a grave" and that "their victims simply did not exist."[14] Similarly, Dr. Jože Dežman has succinctly described the fundamental characteristics of the post-World War II totalitarian crimes in the following way:[15]

> Killing civilians and prisoners of war after the Second World War is the greatest massacre of unarmed people of all times in Slovenian territory. Compared to Europe, the Yugoslav communist massacres after the Second World War are probably right after the Stalinist purges and the Great Famine in the Ukraine. The number of those killed in Slovenia in spring of 1945 can now be estimated at more than 100,000, Slovenia was the biggest post-war killing site in Europe. It was a mixture of events, when in Slovenia there are retreating German units, collaborator units, units of Independent State of Croatia, Chetniks and Balkan civilians; more than 15,000 Slovenian inhabitants were murdered as well. Because of its brevity, number of casualties, way of execution and massiveness, it is an event that can be compared to the greatest crimes of communism and National Socialism.[15]

Table 1: Total number of victims of totalitarian communist regime

Type of victims	Period	Number	Source
Civilian hostages	1945–1990	25,000	J. Dežman (2008)
Total number of inhabitants of Slovenia directly killed by fascists	1941–1990	15,000 (only Slovenians), 100,000 150,000–200,000 100,000–130,000	J. Dežman (2008) L. Sirc (2008) P. Jamnik (2008)
Interned, imprisoned, and deported persons	1920–1945	150,000	J. Dežman (2008)

Source: Author's own compilation from different sources

The communist regime was marked by concentration and labor camps, widespread extrajudicial killings, violent confiscations of property, show trials, collectivization, and forced deportations of the population from their places of residence. Labor camps represent one of the most heinous human

---

[14] Ferenc, Secret World War, 157.
[15] Dežman, Communist Repression, 204.

rights violations of the communist regime in Slovenia. They were first called "punishment camps" and later, starting at the beginning of 1946, "public institutions of forced labor." Apart from forced-labor camps, the totalitarian regime established in 1949 "camps for rehabilitation work," which, in the official terminology of the time, employed "working groups." The majority of those camps were established in 1949–1950, when a number of persons were sentenced and sent to perform socially useful work.

The communist regime between 1945 and 1990 completely suppressed opposition political parties and excluded them from the political process. In short, the communist regime removed political opponents by applying show legal proceedings and distorted legal remedies. This is despite the assurance of freedom of association on the constitutional level and statutory level. The Constitutional Court of Republic of Slovenia described the situation at that time in its decision from 15 January 1998:

> 8. The Communist Party used the political system to square accounts with the urban population opposition and subordinate its wartime political allies. It consolidated power by instituting judicial proceedings against the potential opposition. The main purpose of politically motivated proceedings was to settle accounts with class enemies and confiscate their property. The politically motivated judicial proceedings had many characteristics of Stalinist processes.
>
> Politics viewed courts as their "battle organs" who fought the class enemy. The Bureau of the Central Committee of the Communist Party of Slovenia decided already on March 1945 that they would not allow the restoration of political parties in Slovenia but preserve the unity of the Liberation Front (unlike, for example, in Serbia where Grol's Democratic Party, the Radicals, Jovanovič's Peasant party, etc., operated). OZNA (i.e., the Intelligence Agency of the National Army) controlled the connection of these politicians with the leaders of parties living abroad. That parties in Yugoslavia would not have a future was shown by a series of events such as: the fate of the Tito-Šubašič agreement, the manipulation of elections (electoral registers), the resignation of, first, Deputy M. Grola and then also the Minister of Foreign Affairs, Šubašič, the presence of OZNA at polling stations, etc. What was nevertheless attempted in Ljubljana at that time was to increase interparty connections and contacts with the Yugoslav opposition. This was attentively followed by OZNA; it labeled smaller groups with a common name: the "reaction." In order to fight against the internal enemy, OZNA created a special service: Division 2, with the notorious Subdivision 2, empowered to fight against the interior reaction. Under the reaction, also the so-called remnants of bourgeois political parties were considered.[16] The postwar Yugoslav authorities strived to prevent

---

[16]   Pučnik, J. *From the Archives of Slovenian Political Police.* Ljubljana: Veda, 1996.

contacts between domestic Yugoslav and Slovenian politicians and those politicians who had emigrated or stayed abroad.

9. Soon after the end of World War II, the Slovenian political elite demanded, and the Bureau of State Security (hereinafter: UDV) achieved, a precise supervision of the operation of all political parties in Slovenia. After the first wave of brutal methods, the UDV began to apply subtler methods: multiple interrogations, psychological pressure, threats of legal action, blackmail with pressure on family members or professional colleagues and friends, persecution; in particular, denunciation among people who belonged to the same circle, belief, and party, which was called differentiation. Thus the UDV had been influencing activities inside individual groups, or directing them, and at the same time, informing its superiors and leading political forums (the Central Committee of the Slovenian Communist Party, the Political Bureau and the Supreme Committee of the Liberation Front) about the activities and temperament of previous political groups, church circles, ministries, etc.

10. The Bureau of State Security (hereinafter: UDBA) and the Slovenian Party saw a threat in Christian socialism. In 1949 the UDBA carried out two investigations of Christian socialism and began to follow very closely the activities of individuals from the Christian socialist group. They had been gathering information on Edvard Kocbek from 1946 onwards. In 1951, the Slovenian Party leadership decided to "expel" the Faculty of Theology from the university. On 20 January 1952, they seized Ljubljana's archbishop, Anton Vovk, who was on his way to Novo Mesto; they poured gasoline on him and set fire to him. At the Party's plenary meeting, in 1952, the then-minister of the interior and a member of the Political Bureau of the Communist Party, Boris Kraigher, counted among reactionary circles those "who are in my opinion the most dangerous perpetrators of organized activities directed against us," lawyers, various Catholic-oriented circles among literary men and women, artists and scientists (the Academy of Sciences, the university, and institutes, in particular those that were humanistically oriented), and "the espionage center of our predominantly bourgeois emigration in Trieste and Klagenfurt." On 19 July 1952, the UDV prepared the plan of proceedings to be instituted against Dr. Jokob Šolar. They accused him of treason. The arrest was detailed by the Committee for the Remnants of Bourgeois Parties of the Slovenian UDV. On 24 November 1952, UDBA first arrested Dr. Janez Fabijan and then, on 11 December 1952, also Dr. Jakob Šolar, for their alleged intention to destroy the state and the social arrangement of the Federal People's Republic of Yugoslavia. The court sentenced Dr. Šolar to 10 years and Dr. Fabijan to six years of severe imprisonment. During that time, Kocbek was removed from all political offices that he had held. Thus this was the end of the fight against the Christian Socialists as a political group.[17]

---

[17] Constitutional Court of Republic of Slovenia, Decision Up-301/96, 15 January 1998.

Persons who were courageous enough to criticize and oppose the totalitarian communist authorities were tortured and inhumanely treated and were forced to work in labor and concentration camps. The communist regime also prohibited freedom of expression, and imposed limitations and severe punishment if one criticized the regime. The communist totalitarian regimes created a culture of fear that still haunts modern-day Slovenia. Neighbors spied on neighbors. The communist authorities forced families to rent one room in their apartment or house to persons they did not know and who were, in most cases, spying for the communist secret service on what the family was doing. In this way, the communist created a culture of fear, not only in public life but also in the private life of individuals. Apart from that the communist regime discriminated on the grounds of sex, race, skin color, language, religion, nationality, social origin, and political conviction, particularly as regards the treatment of Roma people in Slovenia. Parallels in inhumanely treating Roma people can be drawn between all three types of totalitarian regimes Slovenia experienced in the twentieth century.

Transitional justice measures in Slovenia

Transitional justice began in Slovenia only after the fall of totalitarian regime in 1990 and it has yet to be finished. It can be divided into three phases. No transitional justice measures were employed after the fall of the fascist and Nazi totalitarian system after World War II. Therefore, one can discuss transitional justice in Slovenia only after the fall of the last totalitarian regime. In other words, it appears that transitional justice measures can be employed during the functioning of a given totalitarian regime, but it is doubtful that they can succeed.

Transitional justice in the transition from totalitarian regime to democracy (1991–1995)

The objective of the Slovenian transition was to achieve a peaceful transformation from a totalitarian communist regime of the federal Yugoslav state into a democratic system of the newly created and independent state of Slovenia. In April 1990 the first democratic elections were held, and non-communist political parties won a majority of the votes. There was no consensus agreed for a radical rupture with the former communist regime. It must be noted that many have called for measures of lustration, which would prevent former communist officials from participating in the public life of the Slovenian state. However, such proposals were rejected mainly by left-wing parties, which are mainly successors of the Communist Party. Perpetrators of totalitarian crimes have therefore not been brought to justice and were left in peace to enjoy their retirement. There was not a single trial in Slovenian courts for communist political crimes committed during the communist regime. In other words, people were given an informal amnesty for communist political crimes committed during that era. Again as in the Spanish case, it was a policy of not explicitly remembering the totalitarian period and its crimes. Equally, there was no truth and/or reconciliation commission established. The networks of the former communist regime were too strong for any alternative mechanisms to be successful. Reconciliation was understood as not mentioning the former regime, as if it never existed. The measures adopted were scarce and only impressionistic. The lack of a clear and well-defined policy in this period can be explained by the fact that another very important task was underway: the transition from a totalitarian to a democratic system and the creation and functioning of the newly independent state.

Nevertheless, officials and judges from the former regime retained their posts, and some remained in positions of power. The last president of the Slovenian Communist Party, Milan Kučan, was later elected the first president of newly independent and democratic Republic of Slovenia. The heavy burden of transitional justice in Slovenia was not distributed and balanced equally. On the one hand, perpetrators of totalitarian communist crimes and those who enjoyed the privileges of the communist regime got away with impunity and without responsibility for what they had done. On the other hand, its victims did not obtain any justice or even recognition and, even today, are denied the right to a grave. This is because the left-wing political parties and successors of the communist regime deny them the right to be buried as "victims of war."

Transitional justice as a partial reparation/compensation for the crimes of the past (1995–2004)

In the second period, the newly independent state of Slovenia had successfully set sail, and it was now time to address the past. Nonetheless, the second phase, between 1995 and 2004, was again marked by the lack of a general, integrated, and inconsistent policy, and only a few measures were adopted. They were designed to remedy damages and redress injustices committed under the totalitarian regime. The Denationalization Act, the Victims of

War Violence Act, and the Redressing of Injustices Act imposed a number of obligations on state authorities concerning the memory of totalitarian crimes. Here the focus was more on repairing damages, particularly those caused by the communist regimes. However, these measures were implemented only halfway. Again, no truth or reconciliation commission was established. No legal act on reconciliation measures was adopted. The National Parliament did not find either a majority or a consensus for adopting a lustration bill.

New developments after 2004

The third period has seen a slight change of the social and political perception of the issues. The first and only case was brought against the former communist official. Slovenian courts refused in *Prosecutor v. Ribičič* to open an investigation into his alleged acts possibly amounting to crimes against humanity. It is not surprising that this decision has not sparked any legal commentary or even discussion from members of the academic legal community in Slovenia. Thus a number of Slovenian intellectuals and politicians share the fear that opening an investigation intocrimes committed so many decades ago would deepen disagreement between different parts of Slovenian society and would hinder the path towards reconciliation between members of the former Communist Party and the rest of Slovenian society. However, examples from other countries show that there cannot be catharsis for the given nation without historically and legally addressing atrocities committed. It is highly unlikely that a single judicial decision can address the "collective trauma" of the past, in which the Slovenian nation was split. However, it may be argued this is necessary as a kind of catharsis to set the new century on a course based on principles of non-discrimination, tolerance, and diversity in the Slovenian society. The handful of reactions came merely from the official media and individual journalists. Most of them agreed that prosecuting persons for acts that were not, strictly speaking, crimes at the time of commission does not violate the prohibition on ex post facto prosecution, since at the time of commission, those crimes were already contrary to fundamental principles of humanity. However, some authors also disagreed with that opinion.

Moreover, the government of Republic of Slovenia in 2004 established the Commission for the Settlement of Hidden Mass Graveyards, and the Study Center for National Reconciliation was established in 2008. All in all, the lack of a coherent, uniform and well-defined policy in Slovenia can be explained through the absence of some factors that are crucial for any successful attempt at transitional justice. First, even now there is no consensus on how to address the memory of communist totalitarian crimes committed in the past. Second, grassroots social movements have started to appear only recently following the discoveries of hidden mass gravesites across the territory of Slovenia.

Symbols of the totalitarian or repressive past (street names, monuments, and other symbols)

Some symbols of the totalitarian or repressive past in Slovenia have been removed. Almost all street names, monuments, and other symbols from the period of the fascist and the Nazi totalitarian regimes have been removed and their traces and relics erased. By contrast, several symbols of the communist totalitarian regimes have not been removed or replaced. A number of statues of Slovenian communist leaders are still standing in cities and towns all over Slovenia. Notably, in the capital, Ljubljana, the statue of Edvard Kardelj, former communist leader, still stands right next to the Slovenian cultural home Ivan Cankar. Furthermore, in April 2009 the City Council of Ljubljana voted 24–4 to name a street in the capital after former Yugoslav communist leader Josip Broz Tito. Also, the cities of Koper and Velenje maintain a street with the name of the former communist dictator. It is true, however, that after the fall of communism, many streets named after communist leaders got back their old pre-communist names.

Youth education measures to preserve and pass on the memory of totalitarian crimes in Slovenia particularly concern the content of history lessons in primary and secondary schools. It must be noted that there are several nationwide attempts to present totalitarian crimes to students and pupils. The history textbooks for primary and secondary schools in Slovenia mention only some of the totalitarian crimes suffered by Slovenia in the 20th century. Slovenian history textbooks rightly mention the oppression by the totalitarian fascist and Nazi system. By contrast, the long-lasting communist totalitarian regime hardly features in the school curriculum. Of course, overt communist ideology was removed from the textbooks and school curriculums; however, a number of communist crimes appear to be intentionally overlooked. For instance, history textbooks hardly mention the crimes against humanity committed by the communist forces in the months following World War II. There is hardly any mention of the show trials of the political opponents of the Communist Party in the 1950s. In the years after independence, there was a prolonged and systematic attempt to wipe out part of their history and culture, yet there was an awareness of what was lost. In short, the old totalitarian ideology and the old mono-perspective about Slovenian contemporary history in history books has not been replaced by a plural perspective about the totalitarian period in recent Slovenian history. A plural perspective in Slovenian history books is required for young people to be aware of atrocities committed on Slovenian territory in the past. More importantly, it is vital to create a national memory of the crimes committed by all totalitarian regimes in the twentieth century on Slovenian territory. In spite of this, democratization brought improvements to the Slovenian history textbook market. A number of small and middle-sized publishing houses started to publish history textbooks offering alternative accounts of the past.

Everyone has the right to a name and a grave. This right exists regardless of who won and who was defeated in a particular conflict. The Parliamentary Assembly of the Council of Europe noted in its Resolution 1481 (2006) that "those victims of crimes committed by totalitarian communist regimes who are still alive, or their families, deserve sympathy, understanding, and recognition for their sufferings."[18] Thus another alternative would be issuing a public apology and constructing public memorial sites dedicated to the victims of the crimes against humanity everywhere mass graves dating from the months after World War II have thus far been found. It must be noted, however, that in 2007 the Government of Republic of Slovenia issued a formal apology condemning crimes committed after World War II in Slovenia. Such memorials could include a list of the names of all victims killed on the particular site, with the publication of these names acknowledging that they fell in the name and honor of Slovenia. What appears to be required are simple and dignified memorials. They would be dedicated to the memory of the victims of postwar crimes in Slovenia. This would ensure a return of civilized norms to Slovenian society. Some monuments and memorials have already been constructed, such as the largest memorial chapel at Kočevski rog gravesite or at Teharje. As early as 1984, Spomenka Hribar raised the question of a public and revered memory of victims executed at secret locations all over Slovenia.[19]

---

[18] Council of Europe, Parliamentary Assembly, Resolution 1481 (2006) Need for international condemnation of crimes of totalitarian communist regimes, Assembly debate on 25 January 2006 (5th Sitting) (see Doc. 10765, report of the Political Affairs Committee, rapporteur: M. Lindblad). Text adopted by the Assembly on 25 January 2006 (5th Sitting). <http://assembly. coe.int/main.asp?Link=/documents/adoptedtext/ta06/eres1481.htm>, last visited 10 May 2009.

[19] Hribar, S. Guilt and sin. *Kocbek's Collection*. Ljubljana, 1987, 11–68.

It seems, however, that each gravesite would require individualist own chapel. Additionally, a museum could be created specifically to honor all victims killed after World War II by the totalitarian regime, which would include testimonies, documents, and photographs to illustrate what cannot be otherwise conveyed and could also serve as an educational institution. This would help to ensure that such acts are not repeated in the future. As earlier generations did not address postwar killings and secret war graves, the younger generations remain obliged to properly settle this question in a manner that will accord equal dignity to all persons. In short, burial sites of all those killed by the Slovenian totalitarian authorities after World War II should include the personal information of victims, the date and location of their death, and the inscription "Victims of war and postwar killings, Republic of Slovenia."

The Slovenian National Parliament amended the Slovenian Criminal Code in 2008, which now criminalizes in Article 297 (2) stirring up hatred, strife or intolerance based on violation of the principle of equality. Thus whoever provokes or stirs up ethnic, racial or religious hatred, strife, or intolerance, or disseminates ideas on the supremacy of one race over another or provides aid in any manner for racist activity or denies, diminishes the significance of, approves of, or advocates genocide or crimes against humanity may be punished by imprisonment of up to three years. This means that publicly condoning, denying or grossly trivializing crimes of genocide, crimes against humanity and war crimes against a group of persons defined by criteria other than race, color, religion, descent or national or ethnic origin, such as social status or political convictions, is prohibited and constitutes a criminal offense. There have not been any cases in which a person was convicted in a Slovenian court for such an offense. However, a number of politicians opined that the totalitarian communist regime cannot be compared to fascism and Nazism. In their view, the communist regime was not entirely totalitarian. Similarly, the vast majority of people claim that the communist regime cannot be included among the totalitarian regimes. Nonetheless, it appears unlikely that anyone will be subject to prosecution for trivializing totalitarian crimes. What is important is that the denial and trivialization of all totalitarian crimes, left as well as right, can be subject to prosecution. Such legislation may contribute to achieving morally equal treatment of the crimes of fascism, Nazism, and communism.

Reconciliation measures

Violations committed in Slovenia after World War II and during the communist regime must be addressed if the reconciliation of the Slovenian population is ever to be achieved. No specific reconciliation measures have thus far been adopted. Alternatively, a truth and reconciliation commission in Slovenia may offer an alternative to the prosecution of crimes at the national level. Thus alternative mechanisms would emphasize apologies and compensation rather than punishment. Such a system may contribute not only to the identification of perpetrators but also to peace and stability in society. Truth and reconciliation contribute to solving conflict peacefully. In this light, W. Schabas notes that peace and reconciliation are both legitimate values that deserve a place in human rights law. They need to be balanced against the importance of prosecution rather than simply discarded. The work of the South African Truth and Reconciliation Commission illustrates that truth commissions can be valuable mechanisms for victims, provided that they adopt and implement victim-centered ideals. In this way, the South African truth and reconciliation process did allow for prosecutions; essentially, people who committed crimes had to testify before the commission by a certain date or afterwards face prosecution. If they did not come forward themselves by confessing, they would be facing a prosecutor flush with evidence. Reconciliation between the different sides of Slovenian society appears very far away. No measures or policies have thus far been adopted to reach reconciliation between perpetrators and the victims of totalitarian crimes, mostly communist crimes. Whereas fascist and Nazi totalitarian regimes and their crimes are widely condemned in Slovenia, there is no unity in the Slovenian political arena in condemning the crimes of communism during and after World War II.

For instance, there is no consensus in the Slovenian parliament to adopt the European Parliament's resolution on European conscience and totalitarianism. The opposition Democrats (SDS) and People's Party (SLS) have requested the adoption of the European resolution also in the Slovenian parliament, whereas the coalition left-wing parties argue that it would be unusual for national parliaments to debate and endorse the European Parliament's resolutions. Deputies of the SDS and the SLS on 24 August 2009 requested an extraordinary session of the National Assembly to discuss and pass a resolution endorsing the European Parliament resolution on European conscience and totalitarianism. Subsequently, the four coalition parties requested on 26 August 2009 that the National Assembly, at an extraordinary session dedicated to the European Parliament resolution on European conscience and totalitarianism, also discuss the amendments to acts on war graves and victims of war.

All deceased persons deserve the right to a grave. Human dignity and respect for the dead is one of the cornerstones of our society. No tolerance is possible without these basic requirements. Those who died as victims of war violence and postwar summary executions deserve inscriptions on the grave that they were victims of war and that they have fallen in the name of Slovenia. Families deserve to have death certificates issued for those killed, and monuments established in the locations of the hidden mass gravesites, such as memorial parks in Kočevski Rog and Teharje. It appears that reconciliation and appeasement between the different sides in Slovenia will not be possible without addressing the heinous crimes of the past. If the national parliament does not condemn the crimes of totalitarian communist regimes as equal to crimes of the two previous totalitarian regimes, the dark chapter of Slovenian contemporary history will remain open for a long time to come. Members of civil society have made a number of attempts to achieve reconciliation between different sides of society. For instance, painter Marko Ivan Rupnik created reconciliatory mosaics in the chapels Pod Krenom and in the Institute of St. Stanislav.

Conclusion

Whereas the fascist and Nazi totalitarian regimes are widely condemned in Slovenian society, the crimes committed by the communist totalitarian regime are not fully recognized by the entire Slovenian society. The awareness of post-World War II crimes is one of the preconditions for avoiding similar crimes in the future in Slovenia and elsewhere. Discussion of crimes committed on Slovenian territory after World War II and secret mass graves is often underpinned by deeply rooted emotions that suppress argumentative dialogue and reasoning and have led to a long-term polarization of Slovenian society into left-wing and right-wing sides. The awareness of communist crimes is one of the preconditions for avoiding similar crimes in the future, in Slovenia and elsewhere. The challenge posed by the transition from oppression to democracy is to account for the totalitarian regime and then rebuild a new society in its wake. World War II in Slovenia was primarily a time of social revolution that saw the forceful takeover of authority by the then-illegal Communist Party of Yugoslavia. In the end, legally, it seems unlikely that any former high communist official will ever be prosecuted by the Slovenian Court for these crimes. Discussion has shown that it is very difficult to show probable cause for opening a criminal investigation into crimes against humanity committed on Slovenian territory in the months following World War II. The issues concerning crimes against humanity after World War II in Slovenia are rife with political implications, and none of the crimes themselves fall within the *rationae temporae* jurisdiction of the International Criminal Court or the International Criminal Court for the Former Yugoslavia. Perhaps most importantly, it is unlikely that the Supreme Prosecution Office of Slovenia will take steps to prosecute more former high communist officials due to the procedural obstacles.

It may perhaps be overly simplistic to suggest compromise on difficult legal and political questions. In the case of crimes against humanity on Slovenian territory, the various constituent groups often do not listen to each other or allow for compromise. Until all politicians realize that some form of justice is inevitable in the foreseeable future, and victim-oriented political parties radically change their ways in asking for nothing but justice, nothing will be done to effectively tackle these crimes. Though the present situation may appear grim, consensus does appear to be growing for meaningful and continued reform, which would settle the question of postwar killings and the secret mass graves of victims in a manner that will respect victims' right to a name and a grave. By showing the extent to which the judiciary and law in Slovenia has (not) responded to crimes against humanity in Slovenia, this report is, among other things, a modest attempt to push for continued progress and possibly legislative reform in the hope that this dark chapter in Slovenian history will be closed once and for all.

Many of the underlying weaknesses in enforcing transitional justice in the Slovenian legal order can be directly tied to the nature of the normative framework, as a coherent system does not exist for addressing crimes of the former totalitarian regime. The main problems lie in the lack of knowledge and understanding among politicians, civil servants, and experts in Slovenia. Naturally, there are many knowledgeable professionals in Slovenia, but the vast majority do not possess sufficient knowledge to respond to the challenges of the crimes of the past.

Identifying the characteristics and crimes of totalitarian regimes is only one way in which the memory of crimes committed by totalitarian regimes in Europe is dealt with in Slovenia. Just as important is the question of how one can respond to totalitarian crimes and how one can ensure that the memory of crimes committed by totalitarian regimes in Slovenia will be preserved.

Judicial enforcement refers to the right to effective judicial protection of fundamental human rights and the right of access to an impartial judge. It refers to questions as to whether human rights have reached the individual. In the Lockean understanding of society, the ability to safeguard one's rights is the cornerstone of society. Victims of totalitarian crimes have judicial access to justice. It is known that human rights are best protected within national legal orders. As in many countries, in Slovenia the protection and promotion of victims' rights suffers generally from a lack of effective enforcement. This explains the high number of pending cases before the Slovenian courts and ECtHR.

Most of the normative framework for the implementation of transitional justice measures is already in place. However, it is not coherently structured. What appears to be required is a clarification of the existing framework in national legal orders. However, until attempts are made to reform transitional justice measures in Slovenia, a vital part of victims' access to justice will remain absent. It appears that the normative framework *de lege lata* is directed towards ends rather towards means. If the focus were directed towards means rather than ends, the normative framework for the implementation of transitional justice in Slovenia could provide some clearer guidance. The current state of regulation concerning the implementation and advancement of the memory of crimes committed by totalitarian regimes in Slovenia is neither advancing the cause of protection and promotion of human rights, nor of the operation of an effective normative framework. The present situation may appear grim; however, consensus does appear to be growing for meaningful and continued reform.

(Un)told Memories: Communicating the (Soviet) Past in Latvian Families

Klinta Ločmele

In Latvia the Soviet regime came to power twice: from summer 1940 to summer 1941, and during the forty-seven-year period 1945–1991. The occupation shaped private memories for several generations as well as the Latvian collective memory for almost half a century. Since the restoration of independence, the younger generation has been growing up without directly experiencing a Soviet regime. Although they learn about this historical period in school, from the media, and through other cultural and social practices, one of their most significant information sources are shared personal and family memories about those times. Jeanette Rodriguez and Ted Fortier argue that personal memory is the cornerstone of collective memory – it is essential for self-definition and for forming the identity of a social group (or nation).[1]

Which twentieth-century events are discussed in Latvian families nowadays? Do they include memories of experiences during the Soviet period? In an earlier survey of secondary school pupils about their collective memory of the national resistance movement (1944–1956), I found that many of the respondents had not learned about their parents' or grandparents' private memories even of great historical events.[2] It prompted me to explore this topic more deeply. Therefore, I asked the same pupils' family members (parents, grandparents, or guardians) to identify the personal or inherited memories that they have discussed with their children in the last three years. Responses show the possible (current) impact of the Soviet period

---

[1] Rodriguez, J., and Fortier, T. *Cultural Memory: Resistance, Faith and Identity.* Austin: University of Texas Press, 2007, 26.

[2] Ločmele, K. Izraidītās Atmiņas: Nacionālie Partizāni Latgales Iedzīvotāju Kolektīvajā Atmiņā. In Kaprāns, M., and Zelče, V., (eds.). *Pēdējais karš: Atmiņaun Traumas Komunikācija.* Riga: LU SZF SPPI, Mansards, 2011, 123–155.

on the process of sharing memories about experiences that were painful, ideologically inconvenient, or forbidden during the occupation.

The current study was conducted in six secondary schools in Latgale (a region of Latvia): Baltinava, Bērzpils, Nautrēni, Rekova, Tilža, and Viļaka. During the 2010–2011 school year, students in the eleventh and twelfth grades (age 16–19) were surveyed.[3] They were asked to take questionnaires home to be filled in by their parents, grandparents, or guardians. Of the 198 distributed, 102 completed questionnaires were returned (52 percent). Maybe some parents refused to participate in the research because they believed the topic was too sensitive. Perhaps they still feared talking about family memories, even anonymously. Before turning to the interpretation of the research results, it might be useful to discuss a few theoretical concepts: collective memory, family narratives, and social trauma.

Collective memory and family narratives

Two elements shape a nation's collective memory: the homogeneous national history and private memories (historical experiences).[4] Collective memory means that a group or society holds a common interpretation of the past, which determines their way of thinking and ensures the group's continuity.[5]

The collective memory of a group emerges because its members remember some event they have experienced. The group owns memories based on private experience.[6] Likewise, some group members may not actually have experienced some events, but they may still have a similar collective memory about them. The primary formative agents of collective memory are textual resources and mediated actions – for example, the media, the educational system, and social communication.[7] Thus it is socially constructed and

---

3   These schools were chosen because of their proximity to the area in which the national resistance movement operated.

4   Nora, P. *Realms of Memory: The Construction of the French Past. Volume III: Symbols.* New York: Columbia University Press, 1998/1992, 632–633.

5   Mead, G.H. The Nature of the Past. In Coss, J. (ed.) *Essays in Honor of John Dewey.* New York: Henry Holt & Co., 1929, 235, 237–238, 241–242.

6   Wertsch, J.V. *Voices of Collective Remembering.* Cambridge: Cambridge University Press, 2002, 25.

7   Hunt, N. *Memory, War and Trauma.* Cambridge University Press, 2010, 97; Fentress, J.J. *Social Memory: New Perspectives on the Past.* Oxford and Cambridge: Blackwell, 1992, 127; Wertsch, op. cit., 25.

discursive, depending on the aim of its creators.[8] Shared personal memories within a family are one of its strongest pillars.

This article looks at family narratives as an inheritance from the angle of communication, focusing on the sharing of family memories linked to Latvian history, especially events and processes that took place under Soviet rule.

According to Harold Lloyd Godall, a narrative inheritance refers to stories provided to children by and about family members.[9] It provides a framework for understanding a person's identity through the self-definition of his or her ancestors.[10] However, not all significant family memories are passed to the next generation. Motivations for silence can vary, although social trauma is one possible explanation.

Social trauma

Social trauma is a scientific concept describing relationships between "previously unrelated events, structures, perceptions, and actions" by stressing their cause-effect coherence.[11]

The sociologist Piotr Sztompka proposes several events as potential causes of social trauma: revolution, radical economic reform (nationalization or privatization), forced deportation, genocide, mass murder, violence, a lost war, and the collapse of an empire. Of course, this list is not exhaustive, and these events will not always cause a traumatic experience.[12]

One of the main characteristics of social trauma is the possession of common, shared memories by a traumatized group or society, assuming that the event causing the trauma does not conform to social norms and should not have happened to them. The group's common consciousness about the

---

[8]   See Gillis, J.R. Memory and Identity: The History of a Relationship. In Gillis, J.R. (ed.). *Commemorations: The Politics of National Identity.* Princeton: Princeton University Press, 1996, 3–5; Kasabova, A. Memory, Memorials, and Commemoration. *History and Theory* 47, no. 3 (2008), 335; Olick, J.K. *The Politics of Regret: On Collective Memory and Historical Responsibility.* New York and London: Routledge, 2007, 26.

[9]   Godall, H.L. Narrative Inheritance: A Nuclear Family With Toxic Secrets. *Qualitative Inquiry* 11, no. 4 (2005), 492. See also McNay, M. Absent Memory, Family Secrets, Narrative Inheritance. *Qualitative Inquiry* 15, no. 7 (2009), 1178.

[10]   Godall, op. cit., 497.

[11]   Alexander, J.C. *The Meanings of Social Life: A Cultural Sociology.* Oxford: Oxford University Press, 2003, 85.

[12]   Sztompka, P. Cultural Trauma: The Other Face of Social Change. *European Journal of Social Theory* 4, no. 3 (2000), 449.

negative impact of the trauma, their shock and fear, and the suspected threat to the society's further existence are inseparable.[13]

Jeffrey Alexander points out that "trauma is not something naturally existing; it is something constructed by society."[14] He further explains: "Events are one thing, representations of these events – quite another. Trauma is not the result of a group experiencing pain. It is the result of this acute discomfort entering into the core of the collectivity's sense of its own identity. Collective authors 'decide' to represent social pain as a fundamental threat to their sense of who they are, where they came from and where they want to go."[15] Thus trauma is not objective but discursive.[16]

The fragmentation and instability of a totalitarian regime after traumatic events does not allow the process of trauma to completely play itself out.[17] Nowadays the reaction to the trauma that was previously denied is a "reconstruction, representation, and working-through producing significant commemoration, ritual, and reconstruction of national identity."[18] Ruth Glynn, a cultural analyst, quoting Bernhard Giesen, writes that the latent period of collective trauma is necessary before the trauma can be "acted out, spoken about, worked through."[19] In the context of this article, it can be said that in Latvia, the latent form of social trauma caused by the Soviet regime existed for the entire period of the occupation.

Social trauma in Latvia

According to Vita Zelče and Mārtiņš Kaprāns, cultural trauma in the community of Latvian collective memory is formed publicly (and often in family circles as well). Unexamined questions concern the participation of Latvians in the destruction of Latvia's statehood, their voluntary or forced

---

[13] Eyerman, R. Cultural Trauma: Slavery and the Formation of African American Identity. In Alexander, J.C., et. al. (eds.). *Cultural Trauma and Collective Identity*. Berkeley: University of California Press, 2004, 61–62; Alexander, op. cit., 86.

[14] Alexander, op. cit., 86.

[15] Ibid, 93.

[16] LaCapra, D. *Writing History, Writing Trauma*. Baltimore and London: The Johns Hopkins University Press, 2001, xi.

[17] Alexander, op. cit., 103.

[18] Ibid.

[19] Glynn, R. Through the Lens of Trauma: The Figure of the Female Terrorist in *Il prigioniero* and *Buongiorno, Note*. Antonello P. and O'Leary A. (eds.). *Imagining Terrorism: The Rhetoric and Representation of Political Violence in Italy 1969–2009*. London: Modern Humanities Research Association and Maney Publishing, 2009, 64.

collaboration with totalitarian regimes and their repressive structures, and the disintegration of basic moral norms during the years of Soviet and Nazi occupation.[20]

The historian Orlando Figes has described the creation of social trauma: "Cowed and silenced, the majority of Stalin's victims stoically suppressed traumatic memories and emotions. …. Stoicism may help people to survive, but it can also make them passive and accepting of their fate. It was Stalin's lasting achievement to create a whole society in which stoicism and passivity were social norms."[21] Figes's conclusion concerning Soviet Russia can be applied to the Latvian SSR as well. Zelče and Kaprāns, commenting on Figes's observations, explain that the principle of silence (and the practice of not believing those nearest to you, lack of true communication, etc.) was typical behavior in 1940s Latvia as well. During rapid political and social change, people learned to keep quiet and taught their children to be quiet as well. The fear created by the totalitarian regime's violence did not disappear when repression ended and survivors returned from imprisonment and exile. Usually former Soviet citizens of the Stalinist period did not speak about their past. The majority kept silent; it was their way of reconciling the existing order and proof of their loyalty to the state.[22]

Research about persecuted people and their families carried out in the late 1990s shows that 27 percent of the children knew that their parents were victims of political repression, but it was not discussed at home. Eight percent of these children did not know anything about the repression. It was only spoken about after the renewal of Latvia's independence. In this way parents tried to protect their family from complicating their lives and becoming enemies of the regime.[23]

It was not only deportations to Siberia that were kept taboo by officials during the Soviet occupation. Other historical issues (that might reveal the dark side of the totalitarian regime or confirm strong national sentiments) were also excluded from discussion. Thus the suppression of memories was one way people adapted to the regime. Analyzing life stories of Latvia's inhabitants, the sociologist Baiba Bela realized that the need for safety made people develop "such strategies as 'silence' and 'forgetting' when the topics,

---

[20] Kaprāns, M., and Zelče, V. Identitāte, Sociālā Atmiņa un Kultūras Trauma. *Pēdējaiskarš*, 19.
[21] Figes, O. *The Whisperers: Private Life in Stalin's Russia*. New York: Metropolitan Books, 2007, 607.
[22] Kaprāns and Zelče, op. cit., 21.
[23] Karpova, Ā., et. al. Represēto Ģimeņu Pārdzīvojumu Pieredze. *Latvijas Zinātņu Akadēmijas Vēstis*, 612/613, nos. 1/2 (2001): 14–15.

opinions, and traditions connected with ideology on national independence and religion were concerned."[24]

The social anthropologist Sigrid Rausing explains that three factors created Soviet citizens' "social amnesia": (1) the intentional lack of memory transmission between generations, (2) a ban on many ceremonies and practices deeply connected with social memory, and (3) the imposition of an official and false history. Historical issues were not discussed publicly or in the family because of the atmosphere of distrust. Insecurity about the expression of memories existed even after the Soviet republics regained their independence.[25] Researching some Estonian communities in the 1990s, Rausing concluded that the oldest generation had fragmented memories of World War II and the Stalinist period that had not been replaced even by the official versions of events. Memories had not been verbalized often enough to achieve clarity in their recital.[26]

My survey provides an insight into the historical events and memories that pupils' parents, grandparents, and guardians in Latgale discuss with them. Research on the family's role in shaping the collective memory of youth in Latvia has not yet been widely pursued, and thus the nature of memory politics in the common efforts of pupils and their families to understand history remains unclear.[27]

Research design

Among other things, the current survey attempts to clarify the experiences of the pupils' families during World War II and the early postwar years 1945–1950. My previous research revealed the first evidence of what is known as "absent memory." Sixty percent of the pupils indicated that they did not know

---

[24] Bela-Krūmiņa, B. *Dzīvesstāsti kā Sociāli Vēstījumi: Promocijas Darba Kopsavilkums.* Latvijas Universitāte, Filozofijas un socioloģijas institūts, 2004, 12.

[25] Rausing, S. *History, Memory and Identity in Post-Soviet Estonia.* Oxford: Oxford University Press, 2004, 93–94.

[26] Ibid., 94.

[27] Several early attempts have produced an article on secondary school pupils' knowledge and collective memory of the national resistance movement (1944–1956) in 2010–2011, and a monograph in 2011. See: Ločmele, K. Izraidītās Atmiņas, 123–155; Ločmele, K. *(Ne) izstāstītā Vēsture: Skola. Mājas. Atmiņa.* Riga: LU SZF SPPI, 2011, 144. This monograph contains some of the research results included in this article. In 2012, a volume in comme-moration of the deportations to Siberia appeared, and in it a chapter is devoted to how the history of Soviet repression is currently taught in schools. See Kaprāns, M., et al. *Padomju Deportāciju Pieminēšana Latvijā: Atmiņu Politika un Publiskā Telpa.* Riga: LU SZF SPPI, Mansards, 2012, 123–132.

whether any family members had been national partisans during the 1940s and early 1950s.

Even if questions about national partisans might be considered comparatively marginal, the same could not be said about deportations. Approximately 60,000 inhabitants of Latvia suffered forced evacuation to Siberia in 1941 and 1949.[28] One-third of the pupils (33 percent) reported having no information on whether any of their closest relatives had been deported.

Why does this younger generation lack a historical understanding of their family narratives? I asked the secondary school students in Baltinava, Bērzpils, Nautrēni, Rekova, Tilža, and Viļaka to take home a survey for their parents, grandparents, or guardians to complete. As a result, 102 of the 198 surveys I distributed were filled in and returned. The questionnaire contained both closed (prompted) and open-ended questions designed to elicit information on the family members' attitudes and thoughts about the history of Latvia and how much of this they had communicated to the schoolchildren.

In this publication I will introduce the public with my findings and conclusions, looking at them through the prism of the social trauma of the Soviet regime. Passive communication of painful memories and those clashing with Soviet ideology remains a typical feature of discussions about history in Latvian families today.

Research results

Respondents' attitudes toward their home country may be a significant contextual factor influencing family discussions of the Latvian state's history. A majority (64 percent) of the parents, grandparents, and guardians involved in my research felt proud of their country, while 25 percent had more negative than positive emotions when thinking about the state.[29]

Perhaps the socioeconomic conditions of the country are a reason for these answers. According to the survey "Eurobarometer 74" (completed in autumn 2010), 59 percent of the respondents in Latvia believed the country

---

[28] Bleiere, D., et al., *Latvijas Vēsture: 20. Gadsimts*. Riga: Jumava, 2005, 317; Riekstiņš, J. 1941. gada 14. Jūnija deportācija Latvijā. *Latvijas Vēsturnieku komisijas raksti, 6. sēj.: 1941. gada 14. Jūnija deportācija – noziegums pret*. Riga: Latvijas vēstures institūta apgāds, 2002, 27.

[29] Twenty-six percent of those responding are very proud to be inhabitants of Latvia, 38 percent rather proud, 19 percent not very proud and 6 percent not proud at all. Eleven percent marked the option "it's hard to tell."

is moving in the wrong direction. The biggest problems they mentioned were inflation and unemployment.[30] Perhaps these perceptions explain why the last twenty years of Latvia's history are only in the fourth position in a list of subjects that family members talk about.

Motives for discussing history in families

The majority (85 percent) of the surveyed parents, grandparents, and guardians believe that it is necessary to explain Latvia's history to their children. Others oppose this opinion, mainly because they think that history is "taught in schools."

Their justifications for holding an affirmative opinion revealed various rationales. First of all, the need to discuss history at home **correlated with Latvian identity** and/or patriotism. For example, respondents wrote: "So the children know who their ancestors are," "for children to know that they are Latvians," and "to teach children Latvian patriotism, which has been inherited from their great-grandparents." The word "roots" was frequently used when referring to the beginning of the nation.

Second, the answers stressed the importance of **creating collective memory**. One respondent pointed to the formation of a shared collective memory: "So the children will know how it was before, how people were deported to Siberia, what life was like in the USSR, because a family is a part of its country." This viewpoint is consistent with another respondent's comments about why it is important to speak about history in families: "To pass on to the next generation emotions we experienced and impressions we had, to compare life now with the past." Slightly different responses emphasize the existence of **different interpretations of social memory**, thus supporting conversations at home as the only way to transmit the "correct" interpretation of history (in the family's opinion): "Because some facts in different history books are portrayed differently." Someone else believed that "everyone has his own opinion."

Third, some of the surveyed parents, grandparents, and guardians used the concept of **Homeland** (*Dzimtene*) as a justification for their views. Sometimes this word was even capitalized, for example "so they [their children] would know what the Homeland is." This was a practice they had probably learned

---

[30] Eirobarometrs 74: Sabiedriskā doma Eiropas Savienībā: 2010. Gada rudens: Nacionālais ziņojums: Latvija, http://ec.europa.eu/latvija/news/press_releases/2011_02_21_2_lv.htm, 23 February 2011.

from their years in the Soviet educational system, or else that they used out of respect for the country.

Fourth, some respondents saw a **pragmatic objective** in speaking about the history of the twentieth century: "So he [their child] would better understand events and would understand their connections." Others provided complex answers that included the thought that **parents themselves did not have much knowledge of history**. Examples: "Even if parents do not know Latvia's history so well, the history of their family should be explained in any case"; "[the children] know history better than I do myself"; "historical issues should be explained to children, but just those whose parents themselves have understanding and comprehension." Judging by the age of the respondents, most of them received their education before the renewal of Latvia's independence.[31] Perhaps the parents' and guardians' uncertainty about their knowledge of history was due to the educational system of the Soviet period. Although some of the respondents had heard about occupation, the national resistance movement, and other "forbidden" topics during that time, others knew nothing about them. The only historical interpretation they acquired was what was taught at school. For example, a 1967 history textbook for pupils explained that the Latvian people voluntarily joined the USSR and referred to national partisans as bandits and supporters of the German fascist occupiers.[32]

These were respondents' arguments supporting discussions about historical issues in the family. However, another group of surveyed pupils' family members have (experienced) a different practice of sharing memories.

The principle of silence

My research suggests that some families still do not talk about history. Most likely it is because of the principle of silence learned during the Soviet period as a survival strategy. The historian Figes explains the genesis of trauma: "The suppression of traumatic memories has been widely noted as a psychic self-defence for victims of repression in all totalitarian regimes, but in the Soviet Union there were special reasons for Stalin's victims to forget about the past. [...] They refused to talk about the past – and conformed outwardly to the loyal and silent Soviet majority."[33]

---

[31] The age of 53 percent of the respondents was 41–50 years old, 23 percent 31–40 years old, 19 percent 41–60 years old, and 5 percent 61–70 years old.

[32] Kanāle, V. and Stepermanis, M. *Latvijas PSR vēsture*. Riga: Zvaigzne, 1967, 208, 242.

[33] Figes, op. cit., 604–605.

Eleven percent of respondents indicated that they found out about some events and the involvement of some of their family members only after the Third Latvian National Awakening (1985–1991), when the Soviet regime collapsed. Finally, the atmosphere became free enough to start discussions (at least within the family) about history and their relatives' experience during those complicated five decades after Latvia lost its independence in 1940. Only in the 1990s did younger family members learn concrete facts about their grandfather's battles as a legionary in the Courland Fortress (Kurzemes katls), deportation, and imprisonment in Siberia, as well as the whole narrative about the family's fate during World War II.

The majority of respondents said that when they were youngsters (during the Soviet period), some ideologically "uncomfortable" questions were spoken about at home. Parents differed in their level of fear of saying something "forbidden," which can be separated into different positions: 35 percent of those surveyed were told not to discuss these issues outside the family circle, while 29 percent were not so constrained.[34]

The summary of responses on the question of why respondents' families did not discuss historical topics concerning Soviet times suggests it was because of fear and the desire to suppress traumatic memories. "People were afraid," "it was not allowed," and "it could not be done as there were 'ears' everywhere" are the most frequently mentioned reasons. Some pointed to the absence of truthful information and emphasized that these events were not "pleasant." One respondent said, "So the children would not get into trouble, so they would not spill the beans." Someone else emphasized a different motive: "Because my parents did not speak much about the offense done to the nation." Another said that family members spoke about such questions, "but little."

A few answers stated that the respondents had little interest in history at that time. A significant comment, which probably demonstrates one of the Soviet-period survival strategies, was that one's opinion had changed for convenience. Some said that the family did not discuss these "undesirable" historical events because they were not "important enough" or not "so topical."

Several of the previously mentioned answers fit the framework of social trauma: offense to the nation, fear, insecurity. The mood in which the Latvian collective memory was maintained during the Soviet period can be seen in this remark: "When Mom told me about many events, she did it very quietly."

---

[34] Others do not remember if their parents enforced any strategy of silence.

It coincides with the concept of a society of "whisperers" put forth by the historian Orlando Figes.

For various reasons, survivors of the camps found it difficult to talk about what they had been through "on the other side," and they closed themselves off from their families. Some people were afraid to talk for fear of punishment (on their release, prisoners were told not to discuss what had happened to them in public, and many thus feared talking about their past in private, too). Others did not tell their relatives because they were reluctant to burden them, or because they were afraid that they would not and could not understand what they had suffered. Parents were afraid to tell their children, in particular, because they did not want to say anything that might alienate them from the Soviet system or get them into trouble with the authorities. Even within families where talk became the norm, parents remained cautious about what they said to their children. Thus Figes characterizes the circumstances that determined the passive communication of family narratives:[35]

> "Even after 1956, the vast majority of ordinary people were still too cowed and frightened by the memory of the Stalinist regime to speak openly or critically" about it. People were afraid to lose their jobs because of their "ruined biographies." There was confusion and uncertainty about the coercive power that could adversely affect individuals, so for "the mass of the Soviet population, who remained confused and ignorant about the forces that had shaped their lives, stoicism and silence were more common ways of dealing with the past."[36]

This somewhat intimidating atmosphere created the context that then accompanied the formation of collective memory for those who are now 40 to 60 years old. They still remain cautious when discussing important events in the past, one of the reasons are the beliefs of parents, grandparents, and guardians that they should not discuss history at home (15 percent). Their insistence that it is a task for the schools probably has a subtext based on their confidence that the educational system will provide their children with the official ("safe") version of the past.

The majority of surveyed family members talked with their children and grandchildren about historical events of the twentieth century. Most conversations, however, usually stayed on comparatively painless topics and not the turning points of the past.

---

[35]   Figes, op. cit., 560.
[36]   Ibid, 599.

The Soviet period – most discussed in families

Collective memory also implies a way in which common knowledge is transferred to the next generation. The psychologist Nigel Hunt points out that an experience shared by three generations plays the most important role in the formation of this concept.[37]

The research results present a paradox. They show that the Soviet period was a time that might have created social trauma for some families and inspired the practice of silence. However, it turned out that the Soviet years have been discussed by 27 percent of the surveyed families during the past three years. Other historical periods have been discussed even less: 19 percent of conversations were about the period of the Third Latvian National Awakening (1987–1991), 17 percent about World War II (1940–1945), and 16 percent about today's Latvia (1991–2011). This frequency ranking might be because the Soviet period in Latvia lasted for almost half of the twentieth century. Another possible reason is that the childhood and youth of these respondents coincided with Soviet control.

History periods of Latvia discussed in family with children in the last three years (%, N=99)

Respondents also were asked to note precisely which events, personalities, and occurrences from Latvia's historical periods were discussed at home (or they could create their own topics). These results are the key to an explanation of the paradox mentioned above. A summary of the responses makes it

---

[37] Hunt, N.C. *Memory, War and Trauma.* Cambridge: Cambridge University Press, 2010, 97.

apparent that the Soviet period reappears in the present in connection with various aspects of daily life, such as the deficit of consumer goods. Actually, itwas the most frequently discussed of all the historical topics of the twentieth century. The second and third most often discussed events concerned the regaining of Latvia's independence in 1991 and the creation of kolkhozes in the early postwar period. The fact that this research was done in a rural area of Latvia may have contributed to the relevance of kolkhoz formation. Nevertheless, two of the three most discussed events were directly connected with the Soviet Union.

Shared personal (nostalgic) memories

I obtained similar results when the pupils' family members were asked to write a few lines about which personal or inherited memories they have shared with their children. The most frequent responses mentioned "the Soviet period" or variations thereof, such as "life in the USSR" and "life in the socialist period."

Some went into greater detail about what the Soviet period was like, the educational system of that time, the job market, and the population numbers. They also listed the Khrushchev period, the 1970s and 1980s, work in the kolkhozes, the deficit of consumer goods, and the influence of Soviet rule in the schools. Some used single words or simple phrases such as "childhood," "the school years," or "the army" when referring to that historical period. Phrases like "life in the Soviet period" and "how people used to live before" could include a wide range of meanings, such as deportations to Siberia, other repressions, and the nationalization of property. But at least what they were willing to admit in their answers is more illustrative of the content of everyday life than historical descriptions.

Analyzing biographical narratives in Latvian local newspapers, Kaprāns has found that nowadays an increasing number of people rate the Soviet period positively. However, their positive evaluation relates more to the 1960s and 1970s than to the 1940s and 1950s, which still hold negative associations.[38] People remember certain decades as good times for them, times when the level of welfare in the Soviet Union rose.[39] Neringa Klumbytė,

---

[38] Kaprāns, M. Padomju Pieredzes (Re)konstrukcija Biogrāfiskajos Vēstījumos: Latvijas Lokālās Preses Analīze (1995–2005). *Latvijas Arhīvi*, nos. 1/2 (2009), 188–189.

[39] For example, people refer to the fact that they had enough resources to travel (within the former Soviet Union) and to afford health and spa treatments at a sanatorium each year. They also mention that everyone could find a job. Medical care was for free, and many

who has interviewed inhabitants of Lithuania in both urban and rural areas, explains that discourse about "better times" especially arises in conversations with individuals who lived most of their lives during the Soviet years. She characterizes the symptoms of post-Soviet nostalgia:

> The younger generations, those who experienced the Soviet period as children or teenagers (the ones in their 20s and early 30s in 2003–2004), usually did not invoke Soviet times as the "better times" unless they recited their parents' views. For them, the Soviet period was bound to school experiences and childhood memories usually colored in pleasant emotions having nothing to do with the symbolic power of the "times." The oldest generations (people in their late 70s and 80s), who had some experience of pre-Soviet Lithuania, often remarked about the differences of the Soviet period as well as comparing Soviet times with the first independence period of Lithuania…. The post-war times were remembered by invoking the partisan movement, deportations to Siberia, the founding of kolkhozes, work in the kolkhozes, tributes, taxes, low/ no salaries, and hunger. The post-Stalinist period marked changes in personal lives usually referred to in general terms: "it got better," "easier," etc. People were able to earn more, they did not face hunger, the partisan movement was suppressed, and deportations stopped. Only the late Soviet times were the "better times." [40]

The Internet survey "Snapshots" (2011) reveals that 62 percent of the 1,072 respondents in Latvia believe that life was better during the Soviet period. Specifically, 34 percent had such a view because of free medical care and education, and 28 percent preferred that period because there was no unemployment.[41] Yet 38 percent of the respondents did not consider life to be better in Soviet times, because "the regime limited human freedom," while 15 percent believed living conditions were worse because of the very limited choice of consumer goods.[42] Increasing nostalgia for the Soviet years is also reflected in my survey in some responses of pupils' family members. Although they mentioned personal or inherited memories of World War II, deportations to Siberia, national partisans, and the regaining of Latvia's independence, their answers more often referred to aspects of everyday life in the Soviet period.

---

had the opportunity to live in state-owned apartments while paying only modest rent. See: Klumbytė, N. *Ethnography of Voting: Nostalgia, Subjectivity, and Popular Politics in Post-Soviet Lithuania.* Pittsburgh: University of Pittsburgh, 2006, 45; Kaprāns, op. cit., 188–189.

[40] Klumbytė, op. cit., 53.

[41] Odiņš, K. Pretrunīgās atmiņas. *Sestdiena*, 11–17 June 2011, 5.

[42] Ibid.

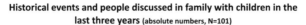

Historical events and people discussed in family with children in the last three years (absolute numbers, N=101)

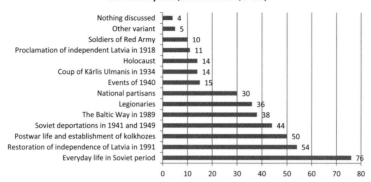

Communication barriers

When asked whether it is easy to speak with children about history, more than half of the respondents answered affirmatively. They added that in their experience, the younger generation listens willingly and is interested in historical topics, but it is hard for them to understand what life was like under oppression. Some respondents mentioned sharing personal memories about Latvian identity: "It is a story about love of the homeland, about many years spent in the Gulag, and many destroyed families."

Nevertheless, 14 percent of those surveyed held the opinion that it was hard to speak about history with teenagers, and 27 percent have never tried to talk about the past with the younger generation. In analyzing their answers, some features stand out. First, from the children they encounter a general **lack of interest** in the past. For example, respondents write that "children are more interested in video games." Respondents also think that pupils are too young to understand history fully, and therefore it does not appeal to them. Such answers suggest that families are passive about communicating their memories. If their children do not ask, these parents, grandparents, and guardians do not raise the subject.

A second feature is the **emotional pain** these family members feel when trying to pass on memories to the next generation. In explaining their inactivity, respondents write that "it is hard and painful to remember" and "it makes my heart ache." Sociologist Tālis Tisenkopfs argues that identifying a negative, abusive action, giving it a name, making it known publicly, and actualizing the traumatic situation is necessary to overcome its diverse impact.[43] But if traumatic experience continues to be suppressed, social trauma will not be cured.

Finally, respondents' responses **downplay the importance of their memories** – "our family is not concerned about it" or "our family did not suffer from deportations." Therefore, personal memories are not communicated, because only the most painful and tragic events are seen as appropriate for discussion.

"Memory plays a central role in both framing national, familial, and personal identity, and constructing the self," notes sociologist Anne-Marie Kramer.[44] She explains that personal biographies and histories are an important precondition for shaping a complete identity.[45] Since 27 percent of surveyed family members do not talk at all to their children about their personal memories of historical events, it is possible that if and when some significant events of Latvia's history are mentioned in conversations, the children still will not know how these events affected their forebears. They cannot fully comprehend the historical context even when information about the educational system, the media, and other social and cultural practices of the past are discussed. They have no subjective experiences that could help contextualize historical events, especially those that have multiple meanings.

Let us take a closer look at the correlation between the results of the pupils' collective memory and the current survey of their family members' attitudes about Latvia's history. Among the surveyed secondary school students, 33 percent did not know if any of their family members had been deported to Siberia (although the apparent awareness in some of the six schools was higher than 33 percent). Sixty percent of pupils did not know if any of their family members had participated in the national resistance movement. These are questions that only family members can answer definitively. Approximately two-thirds of the parents, grandparents, and guardians are sure that their children would know the answer. They are convinced that their children have more information about the family's fate than the children really have. Perhaps this is one reason why respondents were somewhat passive about sharing their personal or inherited family narratives with their children. And perhaps another was the children's inattention (due to video games, immaturity, and so on) when the family discusses this theme.

---

[43] Tisenkopfs, T. Traumas Dziedināšana: Sociālā Rīcība kā Trauma. In Ozoliņa, Ž. (ed.). *LU Raksti. Politika un Socioloģija.* 663. sēj. Riga: Zinātne, 2004, 213.

[44] Kramer, A.M. Mediatizing Memory: History, Affect and Identity. *Who Do You Think You Are? European Journal of Cultural Studies* 14, no. 4 (2011), 430.

[45] Ibid.

Reasons to share memories

Although some families discuss history during their everyday lives, most need some encouragement to share personal memories. A few parents, grandparents, and guardians note that this can happen while recalling some family member or neighbor. But the majority said that family gatherings and the media play a significant role in provoking discussions of historical issues.

Such conversations start after watching television documentaries together. Communication of memories is also normal during events when the generations are together – such as funerals, or Remembrance Day in the local cemetery. Conversations about history happen more often around national holidays and commemorative dates. School assignments, such as preparing for history exams or creating family trees, can also motivate older family members to speak about history and their experiences. Several respondents credit their grandparents for the children's knowledge of family history.

The older generation has direct eyewitness experience and more time to tell stories about their remembrances. If the collective memory of today's parents and guardians was formed by various mediated resources (Soviet history books, whispered stories told by family members, etc.), most grandparents lived through the 1940s and actually experienced the events themselves. (Or at least they heard echoes of them in subsequent years.) Not all eyewitnesses are ready to reveal their impressions, however.

(Un)told memories

This article looked at discussions of history at home as one of the social practices that affect pupils' knowledge and collective memory. The results suggest that memories of the Soviet period are told and untold at the same time: pupils' family members willingly discuss the everyday routine of the Soviet years with their children but are rather passive when it comes to events and processes that had serious consequences in their own lives and those of their ancestors. Perhaps overall nostalgic feelings towards the past are one reason why Soviet times are currently viewed relatively positively in the conversations of family members. Other reasons might be avoidance of awakening traumatic memories, which have been deeply buried for a long time, or simply lack of knowledge to provoke discussion.

Although other social and cultural practices cannot fully replace family narratives, they can do much to promote the sharing of memories at home.

For example, respondents mentioned that discussions about history in families start after viewing relevant TV programs or documentaries. The Soviet (silenced) past enters the works of (qualitative) popular culture. Such works not only bring these issues to light but also provide at least one alternate resource for reading/hearing about events and processes not discussed in families. For example, the Finnish-Estonian writer Sofi Oksanen, in her award-winning novel *Puhdistus* (*Purge*) (2008), described the situation in an Estonian family whose experiences of the Soviet period were wrapped in mystery.

Research carried out in six administrative territories reveals tendencies worth examining in other regions of Latvia, and in other post-Soviet countries as well. This survey of pupils' family members can be enriched by additional research methods, such as interviews with respondents working in other repositories of collective memory – the educational system, media, the arts, etc. The issue of resources shaping pupils' collective memory is essential in a broader context, such as understanding the process of (national) identity formation.

A Judge's Identity

Agata Fijalkowski

Introduction

Two key periods (1944–1956 and 1981–1983) re-emerge in current examinations (1989–present) of the Polish judiciary in the specific context of de-communization measures and in the broader framework of post-transitional justice.[1] In this chapter, I begin with a brief overview of prewar developments, significant to the discussion about the purges of certain segments of society that were set in motion from 1944 onwards. The crimes the chapter is concerned with were intentionally defined ambiguously, so that no one who could be a potential threat to the communist regime could escape. More often than not, the cases, such as political crimes, were allocated to specific courts in order to ensure that the sentence could be secured to meet the objective of the law. The main protagonists in this tale, the law and the judge, play dual roles in the assurance and violation of the principle of judicial independence. The Polish experience supports these claims.[2] The extent of the protections afforded to judges and later transgressions against judicial independence comprise the judicial identity, and both have future repercussions for the judge and the wider profession. The conclusion critically examines selected reforms to show how these challenges to judicial independence are ongoing and of great consequence, not only for Poland but for all states in a post-dictatorial period.[3] While the issues are reflected in its counterparts, my analysis critically contextualizes these questions in the context of the Polish experience. Most examples of attempts to manipulate the

---

[1] For a discussion of transitional justice in post-communist Europe, see Czarnota, A., et al. (eds.). *Rethinking the Rule of Law after Communism*. Budapest: CEU Press, 2005. For a general discussionof transitional justice and its genealogy, see Teitel, R. Transitional Justice Genealogy. *Harvard Human Rights Journal*, 16 (2003), 69–94.

[2] The archival material used in this article is from the Polish Institute for National Remembrance (Instytut Pamięci Narodowej, hereafter: IPN), Warsaw, Poland.

[3] And stable democracies, as noted in Dyzenhaus, David. Judicial Independence, Transitional Justice and the Rule of Law. *Otago Law Review* (2003), 345–370.

judiciary are found in totalitarian regimes, where the judiciary is subservient to the executive will.[4]

While it could be argued that the post-Stalinist period was characterized by a move away from the use of terror to maintain total control,[5] totalitarian rule has various dimensions. In this post-totalitarian period, it is vital to maintain the utmost vigilance, as the technologies employed were such that people learned to police themselves with the memory of the Stalinist regime never far away.[6]

Judicial independence is the "degree to which judges believe they can decide and do decide consistent with their own personal attitudes, values, and conceptions of the judicial role."[7] The judge's position is dependent not only upon assurances in the law, which can include constitutional and statutory guarantees, but also a viable institutional framework that provides for the separation of powers as an essential part of a democratic rule-of-law state. The second aspect of the judge's work, the substantive, entails interpretation of the law. It is in the interest of the citizen to make sure the judicial identity is based upon such solid foundations, because the alternative has long-term, negative implications.

Prewar period

The Polish judiciary came into existence in 1918, when an independent Poland re-emerged on the map. While the Polish judiciary was under the attentive eye of the executive, there is no reason to assume that the Polish prewar judiciary was not independent. In fact, the judge of the prewar period (1918–1939) was augmented by the innovation of the period that concerned the creation of new codes and a constitution. It was a short-lived period in which the constitution and relevant statutes provided guarantees

---

[4]   See Barahona De Brito, A., González-Enriquez, C., and Aguilar, P. (eds.). *The Politics of Memory: Transitional Justice in Democratizing Societies.* Oxford: Oxford University Press, 2001; McEvoy, K., and McGregor, L. (eds.). *Transitional Justice from Below: Grassroots Activism and the Struggle for Change.* Oxford: Hart, 2008; and Stan, L. (ed.). *Transitional Justice in Eastern Europe and the Former Soviet Union: Reckoning with the Communist Past*, BASEES/Routledge Series on Russian and East European Studies. London: Routledge, 2009.

[5]   See Walicki, A. *Marxism and the Leap into the Kingdom of Freedom: The Rise and Fall of the Communist Utopia.* Stanford, CA: Stanford University Press, 1995.

[6]   See Podgorecki, A., and Olgiati, V. (eds.). *Totalitarian and Post-Totalitarian Law.* Aldershot: Dartmouth, 1996.

[7]   Rosenn, K.S. The Protection of Judicial Independence in Latin America. *Inter-American Law Review* 19 (1987), 3.

of judicial independence.[8] Despite pressures placed on the judiciary under an increasingly authoritarian regime, the judiciary enjoyed independence institutionally and substantively, as a profession and individually.[9]

Stalinist period (1944–1956)

Beginning in 1944, efforts were made to systematically dismantle the Polish judiciary. The eastern territories of Poland that were occupied by the Polish National Committee (Polski Komitet Wyzwolenia Narodowy, hereafter PKWN) became their focal point. The PKWN turned its attention to setting up a state framework, which included an administration of justice.[10] This framework had an ideological underpinning (Marxism-Leninism-Stalinism) and a legal model that was ready to be imposed by the authorities. This model was created and perfected by Prosecutor-General Andrei Vyshinsky, who was Stalin's top jurist.[11] In his works and speeches, Vyshinsky rationalized the use of terror in the application of the law as the only true way of ensuring that the criminal law would satisfy revolutionary objectives, which, for most of Stalin's rule, meant identifying and eliminating the counterrevolutionary. However, underpinning the ideological drive outside of the Soviet Union, and into the territories to fall under communist control, was a more calculated intent: to

---

[8] Section 4 of the 1921 Constitution outlined the position of the courts and the judiciary. The constitutional provisions, which conformed to the 1791 document, guaranteed judicial independence (Article 77). Judges could not be removed from office, transferred to a different place of office, suspended from office, or retired against their own will (Article 78), and judges were guaranteed judicial immunity (Article 79). The president of the republic appointed judges (Article 76), while justices of the peace were elected by the populace. In political cases, or in cases entailing more serious punishment, the Constitution foresaw a jury trial (Article 83). According to Article 81, "the courts of justice shall not have the right to challenge the validity of statutes legally promulgated." Since no form of judicial review was created, the power of the parliament (Sejm) was further strengthened.

[9] See Davies, N. *God's Playground: A History of Poland, Volume II: 1795 to the Present.* New York: Columbia University Press, 1982. Judicial independence in the prewar period in Poland is considered in Fijalkowski, A. *From Old Times to New Europe.* Aldershot: Ashgate, 2010, Chapter 2.

[10] The PKWN was established as a temporary executive organ in July 1944 by decree of the Polish National Committee (Polski Komitet Narodowy). The State National Council (KRN) was created by the Polish Worker's Party in 1944. The KRN was a pro-communist party. Definitions of the PKWN and the KRN are in *Slownik historii Polski*, Wydanie III (Dictionary of Polish History, 3rd ed.). Warsaw: Wiedza Powszechna, 1964, 264–265.

[11] See Vyshinsky, A. *The Law of the Soviet State.* New York: Macmillan, 1950.

identify and eliminate potential threats to the communist regime, such as lawyers, doctors, journalists, writers, priests – members of the *intelligentsia*.[12]

The repercussions for the judiciary were serious, because they were not only a target but also part of the plan. This would involve a special type of judge who underwent a close screening process before continuing on to legal education. The screening process was undertaken at different times during the Stalinist period, in a climate of great uncertainty in the administration of justice. Any semblance of stability was quickly replaced, with constant reminders, by the authorities, about the importance of the revolution. Implicating the judge in such an ideologically driven plan inevitably affects the internal ethos of the judiciary to the detriment of the profession.

The Stalinist period was well underway by 1944, and although Stalin's rule would last another nine years, there was notable speed with which the specific initiatives were undertaken to build an administration of justice in Poland. The miscarriages of justice that would occur from 1944 onwards could not have been committed without the complicity of key figures that included representatives from all three branches of government.

Secret sections

The architects of the new legal framework introduced secret sections within the common courts.[13] The work of these secret sections was based on the secret trials and show trials that were perfected in the Soviet Union, where a "script" of charges and the involvement of carefully selected judicial officials (judge, prosecutor, defense counsel) ensured that the predetermined outcome of the trial would be realized. In Poland the secret sections were introduced in the regional courts and the Supreme Court. Within these sections intense pressure was placed on judges by high-ranking political officials, as well as by secret police.

Disregard for due process

Communication between counsel and the defendant was controlled and limited in trials, as was the questioning of witnesses. For example, Brigadier General Fieldorf was sentenced to death in 1950 for carrying out killings of, among others, Soviet partisans and members of the Red Army, in col-

---

[12] Katyn is but one tragic example of this wider policy. See "Russian Parliament: Stalin Ordered Katyn Massacres," Radio Free Europe/Radio Liberty, 26 November 2010, at http://www.rferl.org/content/russia_duma_stalin_katyn/2231400.html (last accessed 9 November 2011).

[13] See Hodos, G. *Show Trials: Stalinist Purges in Eastern Europe.* New York: Praeger, 1987.

laboration with the German forces. This was a crime defined by a 1946 decree, as outlined in the next section. The Fieldorf case, as with the others of that time, represents the fate of the majority of Poles who were members of the Polish underground. This part of the Polish experience was copied throughout the region. Cases were built on the fabrication of facts, falsified evidence, and evidence obtained under torture during brutal interrogation. Archival material shows that the secret trials were adjudicated by carefully chosen judges to reach the desired result, which in most instances meant a capital sentence.[14]

Law

Fieldorf and his counterparts were charged under Article 1(1) Decree from 31 August 1944 on punishment for fascist-Hitlerite crimes and traitors of the Polish nation. The term "fascist-Hitlerite" was opaque enough to use against persons deemed to be a political threat. The Decree on State Security of 30 October 1944 was a repressive piece of legislation that addressed attempts at overthrowing the Polish state and terrorist attacks, subversive activity, and sabotage. Each of the crimes called for the death penalty. This decree was eventually replaced by the 1945 Decree on Crimes of a Dangerous Nature during the Reconstruction of the State. The Criminal Code of 1932 was suspended by Article 68 of the Decree of 13 June 1946, known as the "little Criminal Code." Article 68 of the 1946 decree also established separate military courts, which applied different military criminal and civil codes.[15]

Legal education

As the Polish judiciary entered the post-World War II era, the authorities used legal education as a way to create a legal system that would achieve its objectives. The verification of judges occurred in different periods until 1950. Procedures were created by the authorities to examine the backgrounds of their judiciary. Courts only took on university law graduates and an unknown number of prewar lawyers and, increasingly, graduates from the Soviet Union.[16] In the eyes of the authorities, the weakest group was

---

[14] IPN, *supra* n. 2, file 1796. For secondary sources see, for example, Marat, S., and Snop-kiewicz, J. *Zbrodnia, sprawa generala Fieldorfa – 'Nila'* (A Crime, The Case of General Fieldorf – 'Nil'). Warsaw, 1989; or Fieldorf, M., and Zachuta, L. *General Fieldorf "Nil": fakty, dokumenty, relacje* (General Fieldorf "Nil": Facts, Documents, Relations). Warsaw: Bibliote-ka "Niepodleglosci," 2006, two volumes.

[15] Fijalkowski, *supra* n. 10, 96.

[16] Rzeplinski, A. *Sadownictwo w Polsce Ludowej: miedzy dypozycyjnoscia, a niezawisloscia* (The Judiciary in People's Poland: Between Tractability and Independence). Warsaw: Oficyjna Wydawnicz a Pokolenie, 1989. Also IPN, *supra* n. 2, file 1769, 1399.

university graduates in law from prewar Poland, as these candidates wanted to learn law rather than ideology.[17] Decrees from 22 January 1946 and April 1946 allowed for the creation of a new school for judges and prosecutors; deanships were held by judges who worked in the secret sections.[18] The curricula of the law schools that were set up between 1948 and 1954 were meant to complement the decrees that were passed during this time. The education was brief, and graduates could find themselves adjudicating or prosecuting cases within a year of completing their studies. Indoctrination in ideology ensured that judicial decision-making lost its inherent feature of independence and impartiality.[19] Certainly the period 1944–1945 critically exposed the vulnerability of the judiciary in the Polish territories. Kurczewski demonstrates the manner in which the appointments to the judiciary and secret police were dictated by Soviet functionaries and manuals.[20] Prosecution was expected to conform to Soviet lines, although this institution never attained the status of the Soviet counterpart.[21]

Although limited standards of law applied so as to satisfy minimum expectations, eventually the gradual isolation and marginalization of political opposition allowed for complete control by the authorities, i.e., the Communist Party. Not surprisingly, legal knowledge was not a priority.[22] Corruption was encouraged, and in some cases the judge approached his superior (i.e., the court president) and indicated that each capital sentence rendered had its fee.[23] In his memoirs, the former Supreme Court judge and dissident Waclaw Barcikowski correctly refers to this period 1944–1956 as "rogue."[24] Without doubt, the Polish state of the mid-1940s was heavily shaped by the Soviets. Even the decrees that were issued by the PKWN did not respect the amended law on courts that applied the relevant prewar

---

[17] Ibid., 1399.

[18] Ibid.

[19] See Rzeplinski, *supra* n. 17.

[20] See Kurczewski, J. *Resurrection of Rights in Poland.* Oxford: Oxford University Press, 1993, 31–66.

[21] Garlicki, L. Politics and Political Independence of the Judiciary. In Sajo. A. (ed.). *Judicial Integrity.* Leiden: Martinus Nijhoff, 2004, 126. See also Butler, W. *Soviet Law,* 2nd ed. London: Butterworths, 1988.

[22] Ibid.

[23] IPN, *supra* n. 2, file 1769. Also Stanowska, M., and Strzembosz, A. *Sedziowie Warszawscy w Czasie Proby 1981–1989* (Warsaw Judges at a Time of Trial). Warsaw: IPN, 2007, 25.

[24] Barcikowski, W. *W kregu prawa I polityki* (Within the Circle of Law and Politics). Warsaw: KAW, 1988, 1402.

statutes.[25] The struggle against "the enemy" could easily be imported into a country like Poland, which was dealing with the aftermath of occupation from two powers, making the imposition of the Vyshinsky model of justice less problematic.

The closing of the Stalinist chapter was not without effect. The maladministration of justice associated with the secret courts had a negative effect on judges and public prosecutors.[26] The Party continued to exert control over the judiciary, with respect to, among other things, the legislation concerning the judiciary, judicial appointments, legal education, and judicial terms. The recognition that mistakes were committed under the Stalinist regime affected the Polish judiciary too, although arguably, these effects were limited. In 1956 the Wasilkowska Commission was set up to investigate the secret sections,[27] and its report focused on the most active of the secret sections that functioned in Warsaw, first within the Ministry of Justice. The Commission identified cases in which the proceedings were illegal, where the sentence rendered was simply unjustified. As far as criminal measures were concerned, only one judge was disciplined and forced to retire, but he was still able to collect his pension.[28] Other judges were delegated to the Ministry of Justice, and many of them filtered into the common courts, including the Supreme Court. In sum, the 1956 admissions did not provide any real, meaningful reform in the judiciary.

Martial law and beyond (1981–1983)

As a consequence of all this, between 1956 and 1981, the judiciary did not operate independently. Political pressure on judges continued, notably with the introduction of the Law on the Supreme Court from 1962 concerning appointments to the Supreme Court for five-year terms, one of the most criticized features of the communist judicial system, as it was seen as showing blatant disregard for judicial independence.[29]

Legal education had also undergone another reform in the 1950s. Having an education became important for the authorities, and a certain cohort of law graduate had begun to emerge in the 1970s that had additional legal

---

25 The relevant prewar laws were reactivated on 22 July 1944, but these did not set out minimum criteria.
26 See Stanowska and Strzembosz, *supra* n. 24.
27 Ibid.
28 Ibid.
29 See Rzeplinski, *supra* n. 17.

qualifications, at the masters level, achieved after five years. Most law students who had selected criminal law as their specialization in the judicial route became Party members. Judges who had been educated from the 1970s onwards not only possessed the skills and energy to participate in the reforms that would eventually be set out by Solidarity, but they did not face the internal pressure that colleagues from previous years experienced, as the judges involved in the secret sections began to retire.

The years 1980 and 1981 held a surprise in store for the judiciary, which came in the form of vibrant, vital space, important for the development of civil society. Although this was a slow process and occurred informally at first, the discussion had an extremely valuable role to play in the promulgation of human rights. The evolution of support of the Solidarity opposition movement (Solidarnosc) within judicial ranks is not well documented. A new breed of judge allowed for the reception of the movement and became a logical part of its momentum.[30] This is because Solidarity had already attracted membership within the ranks of the regional civil courts in 1980 rather than the criminal courts. Membership in Solidarity grew very quickly. Likewise, judges were not isolated from regional developments in human rights protections, as the movement in Poland to abolish the death penalty, for example, indicates.[31] While there are debates over exactly how members there were among the judiciary, the fact remains that the movement had strength in numbers in Warsaw. Rzeplinski reports 10,000 members in the Administration of Justice employed 24,000: about 1,000 judges (in courts), belonged to Solidarity.[32] Others state that in 1981, there were 3,096 judges, 867 of whom were judges who belonged to Solidarity.[33] At the center of its work, in addition to commenting on drafts of legislation, was ensuring guarantees of judicial independence. The memory

---

[30]   There was a connection made between the intelligentsia and the working class in the 1970s; after March 1968 it was extremely important, if not symbolic. Students rioted after Adam Mickiewicz's play *Dziady* (Forefathers' Eve) was banned under Soviet pressure for its anti-Soviet tones. The state used this to create conflict between students and the working class, and there was an ugly anti-Semitic bent to the propaganda, which claimed that the main instigators of the riots were members of the Jewish intelligentsia. Gostynski, Z., and Garfield, A. Taking the Other Road: Polish Legal Education During the Past Thirty Years. *Temple International and Comparative Law Journal*, 7 (1993), 243–286.

[31]   Ibid. See also Jasinski, J. Kosciol wobec kary smierc (The Church with Respect to the Death Penalty). *Panstwo I Prawo* 7 (1995), 56; and Fijalkowski, A. Abolition of the Death Penalty in Central and Eastern Europe. *Tilburg Foreign Law Review* 7 (2001), 62–83.

[32]   Rzeplinski, *supra* n. 17.

[33]   Ibid.

of Stalinist crimes committed by the courts was strong, and it came up in discussions.[34]

Martial law

Martial law was imposed on 13 December 1981. It was declared by the Communist Party of the Polish People's Republic. The Council of State (Rada Panstwa) issued three decrees significant to the operation of a state of emergency:

(1) Martial law;
(2) Specific crimes under martial law;
(3) Transfer of certain crimes to military courts, which meant amending the way that the relevant military courts functioned during martial law.

The promulgation of the decrees was in itself unconstitutional (under then Article 31) and was held to be so by the Polish parliament in 1992.[35] All three decrees were published in the *Dziennik Ustaw* (*Daily Laws*) on 14 December 1981, leading to further ambiguity as to when the decrees actually came into force.

The catalogue of offenses introduced under martial law was extensive. The competence of the military courts was expanded further to the decrees. The jurisdiction extended to two crimes in particular, found in the then 1969 Criminal Code, namely against political and economic interests of the state (People's Republic) and public order, as well as crimes listed under Articles 47 and 48 in the decrees previously mentioned, to complement the 1969 Polish Criminal Code, which was already a repressive piece of legislation.[36] Under martial law, the jurisdiction of the military courts was expanded to include crimes that were usually dealt with by the common courts, which were already sentencing persons to increased periods of deprivation of liberty. Under threat, judges were forced to preside in the military courts.[37] Solidarity became a proscribed organization in 1981, which led the Council of State to force the resignation of two Supreme Court judges on the basis that they declared loyalty to the organization. Some forty judges were dismissed,

---

34 Stankowska and Strzembosz, *supra* n. 24.
35 This resulted in the cases brought before the Tribunal of State.
36 See Los, M. *Communist Ideology, Law and Crime.* New York: St. Martin's, 1988.
37 Ibid., 45.

suspected of disloyalty.[38] Military authorities pressured judges in the Warsaw courts to submit names of colleagues who were politically unreliable.[39] As the purge extended to society, draconian measures were accompanied by severe sentencing, resulting in serious consequences for the defendant. During the period in question (1981–1983), the cases that dominated the court workload were political crimes. For example, 62.8 percent of convictions were for political crimes; in 119 cases against 164 persons, defendants were found guilty of contributing in some fashion to Solidarity-related activities or engaging in peaceful protest.[40]

Crimes included under Article 48 of the decree included crimes of enemy propaganda. This comprised several elements, namely the dissemination of information harmful to the state's interests; public order offenses; and disrespect towards state symbols. The category of enemy propaganda was intentionally broad. Usually those charged under this provision were found guilty of possessing leaflets or other material that criticized martial law or called for the freedom of political prisoners. In these cases, the prosecution asked for the four-year sentence, much harsher than what would be proposed under normal circumstances related to public order offenses. An indication of the arbitrary and unforgiving character of these measures was shown more recently in the case reviews that were undertaken by the Supreme Court. All those convicted under Article 48 who had been involved in the dissemination of material defined as enemy propaganda were later rehabilitated.[41] When it carried out a review in 1996, the Supreme Court rehabilitated all defendants on the grounds that it was not possible for such activities to lead to public disorder. In the court's view, the protest materials that were viewed as subversive by the communist regime were regarded as socio-political commentaries, forms of expression essential to a democracy.

Martial law was lifted in 1983, but it was clear that any forms of opposition or dissent would need to be tempered. While the common courts retained control over some criminal cases, it was apparent that political crimes were consigned to military courts. For example, for the period 1981–1983, the Warsaw military court convicted 453 persons in political cases, compared to 192 by the common courts.[42] A number of political crimes were appealed to the Supreme Court's criminal division in the period 1982–1984. These

---

38   See Los, op. cit., *supra* n. 37.
39   See ibid., 45.
40   Ibid.
41   Stanowska and Strzembosz, *supra* n. 24.
42   IPN, *supra* n. 2, file 1769.

cases concerned political crimes that were heard in courts throughout the country. For the most part, most judges in the common courts, when dealing with political crimes, sought to read all files and evidence closely and render a decision that was in favor of the defendant. In several instances the court acquitted the defendant or found the defendant not guilty of the crimes – in this period there were more findings of not guilty for political charges than for ordinary charges. Prior to martial law, a finding of not guilty comprised 2 percent of criminal cases; this increased to just over 20 percent in cases related to political crimes.[43] It is fair to say that judges felt frustrated about the general view that seemed to be held concerning their alleged tractability to the regime under martial law. Deputy Minister of Justice Adam Strzembosz, along with other judges who were also members of Solidarity, tried very hard to rebut this image.[44]

A reassessment of the Supreme Court paints a less optimistic picture than initially perceived. Scholarship in the area confirms that the Supreme Court seemed to support the severe approach taken regarding political crimes. For example, 45.4 percent of the cases confirmed the original sentence. At times the sentence was increased and all extraordinary reviews went against the defendant. Of the forty-five judges who were adjudicating these cases, thirty-five would hear extraordinary reviews. Certain judges' names would appear more frequently, as noted in their average workload, which was much heavier (with an allocation of fifty-three cases) than that of their colleagues (with an allocation of eighteen cases). That indicates a pattern of pressure exerted by the authorities from 1982 to 1984 that points to an informal secret section to hear political cases operated in the Supreme Court.[45]

In conclusion, the new cohort of graduates of a more advanced law degree who had graduated in the 1970s were now becoming judges who possessed the skills and energy to participate in reforms that would eventually be set out by Solidarity. The space was provided for by the retirement of those judges who, despite being involved in the secret sections, had been permitted to adjudicate until retirement, which did not go unnoticed. However, the pressure, threats of redeployment, and disciplinary hearings applied to break the cadre resulted in general demoralization. Likewise, the most repressive period showed the most leniency on the part of the common courts and does

---

[43] Stanowska and Strzembosz, *supra* n. 24.

[44] Los, M. In the Shadow of Totalitarian Law: The Law-Making in Post-Communist Poland. *Working Chapter 9301C* (February 1993).

[45] Stanowska and Strzembosz, *supra* n. 29. See also Kauba, K. Orzecznictwo stanu wojennego (Case Law during Martial Law). *Przeglad Sadowy*, 5-6 (1992), 25–37.

illustrate that a degree of judicial independence can arguably exist in such a regime, where cases were consigned to another, less independent space and where the regime continued to resort to instilling fear in new generations of judges to ensure its will was followed, to the detriment of the profession and contravention of civil liberties and tenets of judicial independence. In this way, the memory of Stalinism is perpetuated.

Post-1989

From February to April 1989, a series of Round Table Talks took place between leaders and representatives of Solidarity and the outgoing government. Concerning the administration of justice, the proposals set out at the talks by the opposition showed evidence of a commitment to judicial independence, which was blatantly violated during these two periods considered above. They included, *inter alia*:

> The introduction of a constitutional provision that guarantees judicial independence and precludes the removal or transfer of judges except for reasons of ill health or disciplinary charges;
> The abolition of judicial terms for Supreme Court judges;
> The abolition of the oath of office required to be taken by judges before assuming office;
> The constitutional establishment of the National Council for the Judiciary (Krajowa Rada Sadownictwa), comprising members from the judicial as well as the executive and legislative branches of government, which would take decisions on future candidates to the judiciary;
> Wider discretion granted to judicial self-government to decide on, *inter alia*, nominations of judicial presidents;
> The selection of members to the district judicial branch from the general gathering of judges from all branches;
> The introduction of terms to the office of judicial presidents;
> The modification of the guiding institutions of the administration of justice and the court practice as laid down by the Supreme Court in such a way that they do not violate the principles of subordination of judges only to the law;
> The creation of judicial benches that are granted the right to directly petition the Constitutional Tribunal in matters concerning the constitutionality of constitutional acts, normative acts, or legislative acts.[46]

---

[46]   Sprawozdanie z posiedzen Podzespolu do sprawy reformy prawa I sadow (Report of the Sessions of the Subtable on Legal and Court Reform). *Porozumienia Okraglego Stolu* (The Round Table Talks), Warsaw, 6 February–5 April 1989, 60–61.

In this fashion 1989 presented judges with the opportunity to form a new cadre, which meant the chance to address and shake off the communist legacy and try to forge a viable, independent judiciary. The Polish judiciary applied the 1990s governmental policy of *gruba, czarna kreska* (thick black line) to itself. Self-cleansing became part of the approach to the past, which meant that judges were aware that not all had demonstrated resistance, and that subservience to the Party had resulted in damage to individual defendants and the judiciary, leading to the naive supposition that "[o]nce normal conditions [were] established, the judiciary [would] cleanse itself of the morally depraved, compromised individuals."[47] Eventually the approach adopted by the Ministry of Justice proved to be fundamentally flawed, as Polish senators became increasingly frustrated:

> The assumption of self-cleansing has not proven correct…it is quite evident in courts…We know that this internal self-cleansing of our courts of law has never happened.[48]

The importance and credibility of these revolutionary changes were undermined by the post-communist government's decision not to carry out a "verification" of judges based on their past records. The deputy minister of justice maintained that Polish judges had tried very hard to preserve their integrity under tremendous political pressures. The Supreme Court was the only court post-1989 to undergo verification and implementing life terms in lieu of a five-year term.[49]

As law and politics collided, the political elite at the time viewed the transition as an exercise in "self-dismantling." In other words, there was no scope to construct new institutions, and without such an incentive, the policy was doomed to fail. The move towards adopting stronger measures ran the risk of being seized by political leaders to support allegations that the Polish judiciary was politically tainted. This would come to haunt the judges in two ways: as part of their attempt to reform the judiciary in response to the Stalinist period and martial law, and now externalized as part of the political campaign.[50]

---

[47]   Los, In the Shadow, *supra* n. 45, 9.

[48]   Ibid.

[49]   Domagalski, M. Sad Najwyzszy zmienil sie przez ostatnie 20 lat. *Rzeczpospolita*, 11 September 2010.

[50]   This debate was begun in the early years of post-communism. Several judges stepped forward to defend their position, claiming to have been following the law. See the debate between the following authors, a lawyer and a judge, respectively: Andrzej Litwak, "Reforma

It could be argued that in light of these experiences, the post-communist judge is or should be even more aware of the importance of and need to address the existence or lack of judicial independence.[51] Perhaps it is time to critically examine how real these concerns are and whether they can be addressed,[52] which entails a reassessment of policies that include the question of unfinished business in relation to allegations of the tainted judiciary that shaped the initial response in the form of self-cleansing.[53] A 1997 amendment to the law on common courts and other laws sets out the conditions for retirement.[54] The amendment is a return to the prewar legislation, in an effort to bolster judicial prestige and introduce stability into the judiciary, with one exception: Article 7(1), which exempted key categories of judges and prosecutors from these privileges:

> Judges or prosecutors who served in the Soviet secret police (NKVD) or other related organs in the 1939–1956 period;
>
> Judges or prosecutors who served the Polish secret police (Urzad Bezpieczenstwa) and collaborated to eliminate persons engaged in the struggle for Polish independence in the 1944–1956 period;
>
> Judges or prosecutors who worked in the military courts in the 1955–1956 period and were involved in the fabrication of criminal cases against members of the Polish independence movement;
>
> Judges and prosecutors who served in the secret sections.

The governing body of judges, the National Council for the Judiciary (hereafter KRS), was involved, as it was a question pertaining to the judiciary. The KRS is a constitutionally created organ, with the mandate to oversee the judiciary, as noted earlier.[55] Seventy-one persons were identified by the KRS as falling into one of the four categories, and proceedings were initiated only to be discontinued, owing to lack of evidence or, in several cases, because persons had passed away. This of course concerns those individuals who

---

... bez reformy" (Reform ... Without Reform), *Wokanda* (Trial Calendar), 14 July 1991, p. 9; Waldemar Myga, "Protest 'komucha'" (Protest of a "Commie"), *Wokanda* (Trial Calendar), 18 August 1991, p. 4.

[51] Bobek, M. The Fortress of Judicial Independence and the Mental Transitions of Central European Judiciaries. *European Public Law* 14 (2008), 1–20.

[52] Skaar, E. *Judicial Independence and Human Rights in Latin America: Violations, Politics, and Prosecution.* New York: Palgrave Macmillan, 2011.

[53] See Krygier, M. Rethinking the Rule of Law After Communism. Czarnota, A. et al. (eds.). *Rethinking the Rule of Law after Communism.* Budapest: CEU Press, 2005, 265–277.

[54] Dz. U [1997] no. 124, item 782.

[55] See Brzezinski, M. *The Struggle for Constitutionalism in Poland.* London: St Martin's Press, 1998; also Fijalkowski, *supra* n. 10.

qualified as judges or prosecutors. In five cases it was proved that there was collaboration with the NKVD; in six cases it was proved that the persons worked for the Polish secret police in secret sections; in four cases the persons worked in the secret sections of the common courts; and in one in the secret section of the regional and district courts and military courts.[56]

After a debate about the meaning of violating principles of judicial independence, a 1998 law, amending the Law on Common Courts, for example, meant that disciplinary measures could be initiated against judges who rendered unjust rulings. Strzembosz reports that thirty cases concerning forty-eight judges were heard before the disciplinary court. Almost all judges were criminal law judges, but only three judges were found to be in violation of the provision.[57]

For Strzembosz, the mistakes of a few cannot justify such generalizations.[58] Some scholars take the position that a criminal trial is the catalyst for self-searching that is connected to the moral limits for the achievement of certain goals.[59] We have seen how judicial identity includes the manner in which the judge comes to grips with the past and how much of the past is present is captured in practice and articulation in the law,[60] where the re-evaluation of the past might even involve a personal or official judicial verification process that can result in criminal prosecution and in a sense freeing the profession from the taint of the past, but equally[61] not to release the judiciary from all forms of dependency, but rather to reorganize its dependency, freeing judges from the clandestine and *ad hoc* will of powerful members of the executive and subordinating them to publicly known and general rules promulgated by elected representatives.[62]

This analysis of the Polish post-totalitarian legal landscape, in addition to showing the repressive nature of the communist laws and regime, it also illustrates the forces that worked for and against the judge and the manner in which the memory is treated by the law will determine the strength of

---

[56] Stanowska and Strzembosz, *supra* n. 24, p. 274.

[57] Ibid.

[58] See Osiel, M. *Mass Atrocity, Collective Memory, and the Law.* New Brunswick, NJ: Transaction Publishers, 1997.

[59] Ibid.

[60] See Glenn, H. Patrick. *Legal Traditions of the World*, 3rd ed. Oxford: Oxford University Press, 2007, 7–12.

[61] And historical record. See Priban, J. *Legal Symbolism: On Law, Time and European Identity.* Aldershot: Ashgate, 2007.

[62] See Holmes, S. Judicial Independence as Ambiguous Reality and Insidious Illusion. In Dworkin, R. (ed.). *From Liberal Values to Democratic Transition: Essays in Honor of János Kis.* Budapest: CEU Press, 2004, 6.

judicial independence and how we understand it. The discussion shows that the past does matter, but not as a determining factor, nor as a deterrent to attempt new and different measures.[63] Generalizations about the judiciary and how the judge will approach her work, under totalitarian or democratic rule, simply cannot be made. Yet political campaigns dictate otherwise, most notably in the period 2005–2007, when the Polish presidency was held by Lech Kaczynski, and his brother Jaroslaw was prime minister; it was during this time (in 2006) that lustration or screening laws were reformed to make them more rigorous. In some ways it was a reply to the failed "thick black line" policy. The Constitutional Tribunal's judgment of 11 May 2007 (K 2/07) found six key aspects of the laws unconstitutional. However, the case of Justice Miroslaw Wyrzykowski of the Polish Constitutional Tribunal (January 2010) is noteworthy for the role of the international opinion and the role in this case of allegations of collaboration with the secret police, charges on which he was acquitted. As criminal investigations and other related enquiries continue,[64] the Polish judge continues to be haunted by the ghost from a short-lived but truly terrifying period.

Concluding remarks

In this chapter I have considered the manner in which two judicial snapshots of two critical periods resurface in present day. I have sought to understand the paradoxes that emerge as we try to construct a judicial identity. Because the respective judiciaries were not permitted an equal standing alongside the executive and legislative branches of power, one of the main points of reform concerned judicial independence. When a judicial identity is being constructed, the obstacle that re-emerges is politics in which practices from the past continue to dictate to a certain extent the manner in which the judiciary reasserts itself. As shown, the judiciary's efforts to reassert itself as a profession following the Stalinist period only occurred when it was provided space through retirement of the former cadre, reform of legal education, and development of civil society. Even during martial law, the courts sought to

---

[63] See Priban, J., et al. (eds.). *Systems of Justice in Transition: Central European Experiences Since 1989*. Aldershot: Ashgate, 2003, and review by Martin Krygier in *Law and Politics Book Review* 14 (April 2004) at http://www.bsos.umd.edu/gvpt/lpbr/subpages/reviews/Priban-Roberts-Yo404.htm (last accessed 9 November 2011). See also Krygier, M. The Constitution of the Heart. *Law and Social Inquiry* 20 (1995), 1033–1066.

[64] See http://www.reed-elsevier.com/corporateresponsibility/hottopics/Pages/ObserverfortrialofPolishjudge.aspx (last accessed 9 November 2011).

work around the draconian measures, and orders were not followed blindly. While relevant laws related to judicial independence have been reintroduced, they become part of and work alongside a policy of self-cleansing, disciplinary measures, the criminal law, and the specific history.

Authors

Jernej Letnar Černič   PhD (Human Rights Law), Lecturer in Human Rights Law at the Graduate School of Government and European Studies, Slovenia, and at the European Faculty of Law, Slovenia

Agata Fijalkowski   PhD (Law), Lecturer in Law, Lancaster University Law School

Ivo Juurvee   PhD (History), Tartu University

Klinta Ločmele   PhD student (Communication Studies), Researcher in the Social and Political Research Institute at the University of Latvia

Simo Mikkonen   PhD (History), Adjunct professor at the University of Jyväskylä

Maria Mälksoo   PhD, Senior Researcher in International Relations, Institute of Government and Politics, Tartu University

Eli Pilve   PhD student (History), Tartu University, Estonian Institute of Historical Memory, research fellow

Maarja Talgre   Journalist at the Radio of Sweden

Silviu Taraş   PhD student (History), Babeş-Bolyai University Cluj-Napoca